THE KEEP
2019

VISIONS OF NEW CASTLE

The Keep: Visions of New Castle

2019 Editors

Susan Urbanek Linville
Stephen V. Ramey

Copyright © 2019 Pokeberry Press

All rights reserved except for brief quotations in critical articles or reviews. No part of this book may be reproduced in any manner without prior permission from the publisher. Pokeberry Press, 41 N. Mercer Street, New Castle, PA 16101.

All individual work published in this collection is copyrighted by the authors, photographers, and artists. Credit for previous publication appears with the works. No work may be used without permission from the author, photographer, or artist.

Cover photos by Bev Martinko

Cover design by Stephen V. Ramey

Interior design by Susan Urbanek Linville and Stephen V. Ramey

First printing November 2019

ISBN 978-1-951847-00-5

Printed in the United States of America

CONTENTS

Introduction i

The Dreamer 1

Sheltered 5

Paper Quilts and Paisley Tears 11

Our Town 19

The New Castle Industrial Railroad 21

Things Are Not What They Seem 27

Heaven on Wheels 29

Line Dancing 33

The Legend of the Pumpkin Patch 35

New Castle Man - Noted New York Artist 39

Hell-View Manor 43

Mahoningtown 55

O Tempo 59

An Invitation to Believe 67

Music in Heaven 71

The Voice of Angels 73

What I Fed My Brother 75

Neshannock Walk 77

On Sunny Lane 97

Nineteen Nineteen 99

Martyred 109

The Gauntlet 113

All Clear 117

The New Way 121

Al 131

Other Books from Pokeberry Press 139

Introduction

New Castle is a western Pennsylvania city that sits in the middle of the rust belt. Like many towns in the region, loss of manufacturing jobs led to economic decline. It is time for that decline to come to an end. Following in the footsteps of Pittsburgh and Youngstown, the city must now rise from the ashes. The Pokeberry Press is here to be one of the many forces that will bring it back to life.

When we were thinking about a title for our New Castle anthology, we wanted something to reflect New Castle's strength and endurance. We settled on *The Keep*.

A medieval castle keep served multiple purposes. The top of the tower was the residence of the castle's lord. The middle floor held the great hall. During late medieval times, the lower storage areas became places to incarcerate political prisoners. Finally, during invasions, the castle keep served as a defensive position since it was located at a high point that could be manned by archers.

New Castle's Keep was created to be a venue for outstanding poetry, prose, fiction, non-fiction, art and photography by novices and professionals. The only constraint is that the subject matter includes New Castle, PA in some way, be it past, present or future.

We hope you enjoy the first of many anthologies to come.

The Dreamer

Lavonne Lyles

I told the whole world what I knew was a lie,

that I was a dancer whose fame reached to the sky.

I had them believing my dance was supreme,

but deep down I knew, it was only a dream.

Only a dreamer, that's all you see, only a dreamer of what I could be.

Jesus, my Father, I cry and I plea,

Make my next dream a reality.

City of New Castle, thank you for making my dream come true. Lavonne Lyles is affectionately known as New Castle Cane Lady.

Susan Urbanek Linville

*New Castle's famous "Cane Lady",
Lavonene Lyles poses before a mural at
the Pokeberry Exchange.*

Sheltered

Debra R. Sanchez

As the owner of a small independent publishing company, I often participate as a vendor at regional markets, festivals, and conferences. While returning home from one such event a few weeks ago, I came across a detour on my usual route. My phone's GPS kept insisting that I follow certain directions. I knew the instructions that blared from the all–knowing Google Maps voice would indeed get me where I wanted to go.

However, this part of the world, rural Lawrence County, is where I grew up. It's where I learned to drive. It's where my heart lives. So, I went the way I wanted to go. I created my own personal detour, meandering through some of my favorite places, seeking the landmarks that I wanted to revisit.

Places of my youth.

Places of my dreams.

Places of my nightmares.

Four–and–a–half decades ago, my brother and I used to wade in the creek that flowed in front of our home in Eastbrook, catching frogs, tadpoles, and mosquito bites. We played in the woods up the hill that loomed around the house and the abandoned cottage on the same property.

In summer, we explored every inch of that cottage. Broken floorboards and crumbling walls were dangers we ignored. So were the raccoons, rats, snakes, and who knows what else that had taken up residence there.

In winter, we rode our sleds down a narrow path, careening through the trees, risking life and limb for the thrill. That's as far into the woods as my brother would go. Not me.

For the three years that we lived in that house, unless it was raining, I spent almost every waking moment that I wasn't in school up in the woods. I built a primitive shelter, sturdy and well stocked. I made the furniture from branches, bark, and rocks. I did my homework there. I was nose–to–nose with a deer a few times. It was my own castle, my own keep. No one but me knew it existed.

The woods belonged to me, no matter who owned the property.

Not far from my shelter there was a round clearing. In time, I thoroughly explored the woods on the other side. There was an old stone foundation that had been taken over by the hilltop swamplands. To the side of the former homestead, a circle of flat-topped stones surrounded what appeared to be a shallow pond smothered in lily pads and scummy water. I felt drawn to the lonely disintegrating fireplace and shadows of walls that used to be.

I constructed a new hideaway. My new shelter was close enough to bask in the bog music, yet far enough away to stay dry.

On the other side of the woods was Devil Elbow's Road.

It was there that I learned to fear the truth. One day, while I was reading, I heard voices.

Until that moment, I had never seen or heard a soul in those woods. They were coming, obscurely chanting.

I knew to stay out of sight. My shelter worked well. I watched without being seen. The robed chanters passed within a few feet, close enough to smell them. I will always remember that scent, but I have yet to identify it. I heard their ritual in the clearing, saw the flashes, tasted the smoke, and smelled the blood.

I waited until they retraced their path, chanting in reverse. When they were out of sight and sound, I made my way home.

It was moonless dark by then, but I knew my way around those woods. I also knew my mother would be worried. I hoped she would be worried enough that she would be relieved to see me.

She wasn't.

I'm certain that I could have negotiated my way out of the "two weeks, no woods," if I had tried. I'm even more certain that if I had told the truth about what I witnessed, the "two weeks" grounding would have turned into "FOREVER!"

I never saw or heard anything like that again. A few months later we moved a mile up the road. Although it wasn't far, and I explored other woods and fields, I never returned to the clearing. I never built another shelter. I could though. I know I could. Even now.

The day of the detour I almost went up that road. A friend was following me, though, and might have been more lost and confused if I had done so. I confessed my temptation over our lunch at a castle–like restaurant in a nearby town.

That memory of so long ago is crisp and clear as well as faded. I cannot be certain that the events I so vividly remember happened. It is entirely possible that I fell asleep while reading that day. My imagination has always been my strength and my weakness.

Who can really tell what is and is not real?

Rowin Collins

Pearson Park, January 1st, 2019

Paper Quilts and Paisley Tears

Jere Moon

I once had the perfect life in New Castle, Pennsylvania. My husband and I had a Cape Cod home in a friendly East Side neighborhood. We had two wonderful children, Franklin and Christy. Franklin, our youngest, was a computer whiz. Christy was beautiful and held a master's degree in psychology. She had the world by the tail, or so we thought.

Christy was only twenty–six when she took an entire bottle of narcotics prescribed by her doctor for back pain. We found her unresponsive in her white–framed bed beneath the pink floral quilt I had made for her twenty–first birthday. Her death cast our family into a whirlwind.

Franklin, unable to deal with his grief, joined the army. It only created more loss for me and my husband. We prayed every day that he would return alive and uninjured.

Four years later, Franklin completed his military service and got married. We grew to love his wife, Valorie, like a daughter. Over the next twenty years, we became a happy family again.

And then one evening we got a phone call from our daughter–in–law. She was crying hysterically.

"Franklin collapsed on the kitchen floor. We're at Jameson Hospital. They think he had a stroke." Medical machines beeped in the background. "Get here as fast as you can. The doctor doesn't think he'll make it."

"He's only forty-two," I said. "He's too young to have a stroke."

"Hurry," she begged.

"We're on our way."

My husband was already at the door with the car keys. He drove us to the hospital as fast as he could.

We rushed to the emergency room and pulled back the curtain around Franklin's bed. One long beep sounded. The doctor listened with his stethoscope.

"I'm sorry," he said. "It was a massive stroke. We did everything we could." He paused with a look of sympathy, mixed with failure. He lost a patient. We lost our only remaining child.

A petite blonde nurse quickly detached wires and tubes from my son's lifeless body. I longed to take Franklin into my arms, hug him, and tell him I loved him, but memories of Christy's icy limbs stopped me. I couldn't touch another dead child. I wanted only to remember Franklin's warmth, the way he felt and smelled on that cold December day when he was born.

"Take as much time as you like," the nurse said. She threw used alcohol wipes into the trash and adjusted the sheet up to Franklin's chin. "Let us know if you need anything."

The moment she stepped out, a guttural cry erupted from deep within me, the same sound I made the day I found Christy. All those years I kept Christy's bedroom like a mausoleum, door closed to conceal my grief. Now it burst open with raw emotions. A blend of old tears for Christy, fresh ones for Franklin.

My husband and Valorie cried too. Our pain was so great we couldn't comfort each other.

Finally, Valorie wiped her eyes, closed the curtain, and gave the appropriate funeral information to the nurse at the desk. Numbly, the three of us walked to our cars.

We followed Valorie home. Home—the place where Franklin lived when he was alive.

"Do you want us to stay with you?" I asked.

"No, I'll be all right. Get some rest. I'll call you in the morning."

I tossed and turned all night. Every time I managed to doze, I would shudder myself awake. Franklin was dead. My only consolation was knowing Christy and Franklin were together again. They had a close relationship here on Earth. Now it could continue.

Shortly after Franklin's funeral, Valorie informed us she would be moving out of town to be near her side of the family. For us, it was yet another loss.

As time went on, I felt myself slipping away. I slept a good part of my days, unable to cook, clean, or do much of anything. My friends said I was depressed and urged me to see my doctor. It didn't help that my husband was dealing with a serious lung infection.

I took their advice. The doctor prescribed an antidepressant. It didn't help. I slept even more. I started having trouble with my vision and balance, and although I never admitted it, I was falling for no apparent reason. One accident resulted in a nasty gash to my forehead. My husband rushed me to the Emergency Room at Jameson where they stitched me and did an MRI to make sure I didn't have a concussion.

We were preparing to leave, when the doctor hurried in. "Your scan shows a fairly large brain tumor. It must be removed as soon as possible. I'm sending you by ambulance to a neurosurgeon at Montefiore in Pittsburgh. Your family can meet you there."

"We have no family," I said. It was true. And because of that, I didn't care if I lived or died. But for some reason, I asked God to help me.

My husband followed the ambulance. Together, we confronted the serious–looking Montefiore doctor.

"A benign frontal tumor," he said.

I froze at the words.

The men talked as if I wasn't there. "Benign" my husband said. A coughing fit overtook him. "That's good, isn't it?"

"It's not cancerous, but this kind of tumor can create all kinds of problems. I can remove it in pieces through her nasal passage to mitigate trauma to her brain. I'll do the surgery first thing in the morning."

It felt like I was in a bad dream. Somehow, I signed the consent forms.

I don't remember anything after that. My husband said my surgery lasted twelve hours. Unfortunately, the doctor couldn't remove the entire tumor. I would need more surgery when the mass started to grow again. He suggested I go to a nursing home to recover since my husband's ailment had been diagnosed as a serious and chronic lung condition. He would have trouble caring for me on his own.

My husband found a facility in our neighborhood, The Haven Convalescent Home. I arrived by Noga ambulance in a confused state. I thought the Haven was my house.

"It was nice of you to move the bird feeder in front of the window so I can watch the birds," I said. "But what did you do with my easy chair?"

I believed the staff members were family or neighbors and I literally called them by those names. I ignored name tags and renamed them, from the cook to the administrator.

"Don't get smart with me, Richard Peter Browly," I said when a tall male aide with glasses corrected his name. "I know who you are. You're my nephew." In my mind, he was. You should have heard the fuss I made when he tried to take me to the bathroom.

A few days later, I asked my husband, "Where's Mother?"

He sucked from an inhaler. "She died."

I gasped. "Why didn't someone tell me?"

"Your mother died ten years ago. I took you to her funeral at R. Cunningham's on Wilmington Road. Don't you remember?"

It took several days to convince me that Mother was dead, but finally I retained the information.

'Where's Christy? Sara's been here several times today looking for her." I had labeled the bubbly, dark–haired aide as my daughter's childhood friend.

"Christy overdosed on pain pills," my husband said tightly. "She died before your mother."

"No! Christy would never do that. She's too smart."

The next day I asked about Christy again, and like before, my husband told me the same tragic story.

"Is Franklin in his room reading comic books? You have to look under his pillow He keeps a flashlight there."

"Franklin died last spring from a stroke. We didn't make it to the hospital in time to see him, remember?"

"His poor wife," I said. "Is she all right?"

"Valorie moved away to be near her parents."

"We have no family?" A voice echoed inside me. I knew it was true.

My husband kissed me gently. "We have each other. We'll be okay."

Several days later, I received my first get well card. It was signed, 'The Library Stitchers.'

"Strange," I said. "I don't know who it's from. We don't live on Paul Street."

"It's from your quilting group," my husband said. "You're in a nursing home on Paul Street, recovering from brain surgery."

I looked over my glasses. "Convalescent Home," I corrected. I only knew that because that's how it was addressed on the envelope. I struggled to get out of my wheelchair but couldn't. "We better get home and let the dog out."

"Barney died several years ago," my husband said.

I sighed. "I'm going to stop talking to you. All you do is tell me everyone's dead."

Physical therapy was just as confusing. I couldn't remember how to walk or dress myself.

I was about to give up when a friend came in. It was good to see a familiar face. I even remembered her name—Mary. Mary was a nurse and had taken care of her mother for years before she passed away.

She encouraged me to take a step. I didn't want to let her down, so I tried until I did it. She clapped with excitement like I was a child, and for some strange reason I was also excited over my simple accomplishment.

The next day, she brought me a plaque that said: *No path is too difficult if you walk with a friend.* She also brought chocolate—my favorite food. I gulped it down. That day in therapy, I took a few more steps.

Mary came almost every day and assured me I was doing well. It would take time to regain my strength. She also brought me an adult coloring book and crayons to help ease my stress and improve my coordination.

I looked at the pictures. "They're very nice, but I don't want to color. You do it."

"You like to quilt," Mary said. "What colors would you pick if this was a quilt?" Without hesitation, I chose harmonizing pinks and greens. But I made my friend color the flowers.

That evening, after my husband and Mary left, I got lonely. I asked several workers if they'd color with me. They enjoyed it and said it eased their frustrations. From then on, I invited them to join me on their breaks, or whenever they had time. My room had a constant flow of traffic and stimulating conversations. I ended up with lots of pretty pictures. An activity aide suggested I glue them together to look like a quilt wall hanging.

During the next week, I arranged the prints into various patterns on my bed. With each twist and turn, memories of quilting eased their way into my head.

"Now I remember!" I told my husband. "I am the *organizer* of The Library Stitchers." This brought a burst of renewed confidence.

Mary suggested punching holes around the pictures and stitching them together with yarn.

"Bring in my sewing basket," I said to my husband. "It's next to my easy chair." The following day he brought it. Everyone, including me, was surprised to learn it was exactly where I had told him.

Mary offered to help even though she wasn't a quilter, or much of a sewer. I had to show her how to do a basic stitch and simple French knot. While we sewed, I learned she liked to hike. She had just walked the trails at Cascade Park before she came to see me.

I smiled. "We used to take Christy and Franklin there for a picnic on the last day of school." I nodded to my husband. "Remember, Honey?"

My husband and Mary were happy I was remembering more of my past, but I wasn't so pleased with my friend's sewing skills. Mary's stitches were crooked.

"Bring in my seam ripper," I said to my husband as soon as she left. "It's next to my sewing machine."

It was exactly where I told him.

If Mary noticed her sewing had been redone when she returned the next day, she didn't let on. I was hoping she'd do better on the next square, but she was more focused on describing her hike in Moraine State Park.

"I remember when that lake was built," I said, dipping my needle through the punched holes of my paper quilt. "My husband and I bought a pontoon boat. We had a lot of fun there."

My husband smiled. I could almost hear our children's laughter as they threw pieces of bread to the screeching seagulls. Unfortunately, I also remembered Christy and Franklin were gone. Blinking back a tear, I handed my husband a needle to thread. He had bad lungs, but really good eyes.

The next week, Mary talked about hiking at McConnell's Mill. It stirred up more memories.

"I remember taking a family photo in front of the Red Covered Bridge," I told her. "Even Mother was in it. In her day, folks took wheat there to be ground into flour."

With each quilt square, I was remembering more, but I hadn't noticed that my husband's health was declining. Visiting me every day was wearing him down. I later found out that Mary had to take him to the hospital several times during my stay. Each episode left him weaker.

On my nine–month check-up, the doctor said my tumor wasn't growing. I had made such great improvement that I could go home. I was excited at the prospect of living a normal life again.

The day I was to be discharged, my husband took a bad spell and died.

A month after his funeral, I sold our house and moved into an assisted living apartment with a nook for my sewing machine. I hung my paper quilt on the wall in front of my easy chair.

That quilt reminds me how fragile life is, that, at any moment, the stitches that hold our world together can be ripped apart. Whenever I get lonely, I look at it, and remember the needles my husband, the happy times I spent coloring with workers at the Haven.

On Mary's last visit, she suggested I make a grieving quilt. "A real quilt." At the time it was the last thing I wanted to do. Now, when she arrives to check up on me, I pick shades of pink and green fabric.

I cry so hard making the first square that my stitches are crooked. This time it is Mary who rips out and redoes *my* stitches. I must admit her sewing is improving.

By the fourth block, I wipe away my paisley tears. I know from past traumatic experiences that I can get through this.

Mary hands me a piece of chocolate. "No path is too difficult if you walk with a friend." I pull my needle through the fabric and imagine how beautiful the quilt will look when it's finished.

Our Town

Robert Stull

Remember when you could walk through this town
With so many people and stores all around
In the summer, the fairs and Cascade Park,
And feeling safe to be out after dark
There was always something going on in our city
But it's now like a ghost town and it sure is a pity.

Tear everything down and look what we got
Dollar stores, pharmacies and parking lots
Though some tried to bring the festivities back,
As the years went by, the interest went slack
The "Fireworks Capital," New Castle PA
Now we are lucky if we even see a display.

It seems no one is willing to step to the plate
To try to get back what once made our town great
Yes, remember how we used to do things among us,
The good times and memories and feelings of trust
The past generations were great to grow up in
Remember "Our Town," before it was worn thin?

The New Castle Industrial Railroad

Kat Burg

Necessity is the mother of invention, the spark for an idea which gives impetus to a successful entrepreneurship.

By the late 19th and early 20th Centuries, New Castle had grown into a major center of industry and steel. In addition, it was touted for mining coal and limestone, and manufacturing cement, glass, pottery, and tin. Immigrants located in the area for the surplus of jobs as the economy boomed.

In the late 1970's, the U.S. steel industry collapsed. This caused a negative impact on railroad services across the nation. Mergers, sales, and abandonments left New Castle with local railroads ceasing operations and creating new subsidiaries. These Class I lines focused on long-distance mainline routes for revenue.

The Pittsburgh & Lake Erie Railroad (P&LE) was almost out of business and CSX and Conrail had curtailed service to marginal accounts. CSX included the Chessie System Railway and the Seaboard Coast Line Railway. The 'X' stood for non-transportation subsidiaries, such as resort, video production, and mineral companies acquired in merger. An artificial acronym came into wide use: 'Can't Say eXactly.'

Dale Berkley, Sr. had worked for P&LE through their steady decline from 1968 to 1992. Now, he saw a golden opportunity. New Castle's industrial base would become non-existent without reliable rail service. He couldn't let that happen. With a small group of area investors, he started a short line railroad. Interchange Specialty Services Rail became a class III common carrier.

The industrial short line would accommodate and salvage the businesses that remained in operation, such as Adams Manufacturing, Bridges & Towers, Double R. Plastics, Ellwood Mill Products. Ellwood Quality Steel, Ferrotech, Hilti, Hobel Salvage, New Castle Recycling, North American Forgemasters, and Slippery Rock Salvage. Dale realized the potential for New Castle's industry to prosper into the future. Connecting these industries to two major Class I rail carriers, the Norfolk Southern and CSX, was key.

Dreams don't always happen overnight. In 1992, Dale took a severance pay from the faltering P&LE, mortgaged his residence, and risked it all. It took brains and brawn to ready the rail line and bring plans to fruition. Through blood, sweat, and tears, his group repaired, replaced, and built new rail.

They purchased discontinued tracks put out of service when former steel and tin industries closed. They also acquired rights to serve area steel producers and scrap processors, and to begin an interstate common carrier service with any interested shippers along his rail line.

As a class III common carrier, tracks are required to be maintained and meet the standards of the Federal Railroad Association. This was not an easy process, but Dale's group persevered. His vision transformed into a viable short line, a lifeline for local businesses—a dream come true for many.

In the late 90's, to avoid confusion and red tape over two similarly named entities, ISS Rail became New Castle Industrial Railroad (NCIR). By 2001, it existed as an independent operation with Dale Sr. serving as President, and Randy Knox as Vice-president.

Up popped the 1,600 square foot, blue metal headquarters inscribed with the business name at 702 Moravia Street. The top level serves as office space. The ground floor houses up to four engines for minor repairs and keeps them above 59 degrees during cold weather. This nugget of railroad quickly became a priceless pearl living in a blue oyster.

"It was one of the best-kept secrets in town," Dale said.

Dale Sr. currently employs nine people at a good salary, including railroad retirement benefits. Each is certified as a locomotive engineer. They attend ongoing courses and certifications in operation safety, Hazmat Rail and Air Brake Training.

New Castle Industrial Railroad's hours of operation accommodate the needs of their rail-shipping customers. NCIR welcomes new shippers to locate within their right-of-way. Through teamwork, and the two major railways accessing the area, products reach all major markets across

North America. In addition, the Buffalo Pittsburgh Railroad travels from New Castle to Buffalo, New York.

Today, the short line industrial switching district in New Castle services approximately twenty accounts along its twenty miles of track. They include Adams Manufacturing, Amco Plastics, American Rock Salt, Ben Weitsman Recycling, Consolidated Containers, Covanta, Dura Edge Products, EMP, New Castle EQS, Hill Railcar, Hobel Brothers Scrap, Kasgro Rail, Morton Road Salt, New Castle Recycling, North American Forgemasters, PSC Metals, RWE Transload Facility, Shell Oil Railcar Storage and Distribution, and Silgan Ipec. Another Ellwood Quality Steel mill is under construction. This steel vacuum remelt facility is part of the Ellwood Steel Group.

Initially, there were six financial partners, but Dale eventually became sole owner. Now, NCIR exists as a family business with two of his sons at the helm of daily operations. Dale Jr., the Vice-president, graduated from Union High School and Houghton College with a business degree.

After graduating, Junior worked for CSX in New Castle and Jacksonville, Florida, but NCIR is in the family blood. He left his position, experienced and ready to help his father with the short line business.

The V.P. of Operations, grandson Deven, graduated from Slippery Rock University with a business finance degree and a minor in Bio-Chemistry. He is a certified FRA track inspector.

The family understands the industry and how a short line connects a concentrated, thriving industrial corridor where larger Class I carriers don't go. Without this unique service, businesses would close, relocate, and hundreds of interconnected jobs would disappear from New Castle.

Dale's wife, Peggy, retired as a state health nurse. Their other son, Darren, a teacher, resides out of state. As far as retirement plans go, Dale says, "I officially retired three years ago." He enjoys travel but spends ample time at the business. His vocation turned into an avocation.

The powerhorses of the operation are their three locomotives. These 1,500 horsepower EMD switching units boast superior traction and pulling power. They are painted NCIR's red, black, and white paint scheme in honor of the New Castle School District.

NCIR once offered public caboose rides and participated in community events, such as the annual Mahoningtown Community Day Festival in August. As part of November's Christmas parade in downtown New Castle, NCIR once fashioned a Santa train. Public safety, insurance, and liability curtailed that involvement. However, many people treasure those memories.

The Berkleys take great pride in the cleanliness, reliability, and operation of their business. The short line remains a catalyst for the community as well as economic growth in the industrial hub of New Castle. Business may come and go, but NCIR remains rooted, productive and prosperous.

Kat Burg

Photo 1: Owner Dale Berkley, Sr. proudly stands with Conductor Greg Smock on NCIR's 1500 horsepower switching unit locomotive, the EMD. Photo 2: Conductor Dan Wilson sits in his switcher locomotive prepared for a productive day.

Things Are Not What They Seem

Colleen Seeger

I remember driving by this block in New Castle as a little girl and the entire expanse blazed with lights. It was Christmas and the circus rolled together into something I couldn't describe as other than exciting.

I asked my Mother what the pretty place was, and she smiled with some sadness. "Rich people go there. We will have to wait a long time for our chance. But maybe you'll get in, Sweetie. Someday. Tell me all about it when you do."

I thought she had a plan and would let me know when we got rich. I didn't ask her about it. She would surprise me when that day came. I imagined tea parties and princesses, fluffy little dogs doing tricks, and very kind grandmothers passing out cookies. I was four years old.

We didn't drive by that block very often, but it remained fascinating to me. When I was six, life took me far from those magical buildings. My father went on a trip, and I never saw him again. Not much was said to me at the time and as I got older my questions received only vague answers. Father wasn't dead, but as to where he was, well, that was the dark mystery. *He's doing top secret work and only my mother knows where he is,* was the story I told my friends at school. It gave me a feeling of being special. I stopped telling that story when I was ten. Nobody believed it anyway.

Just before I turned sixteen, things changed quickly. Mother was no longer so somber. She became talkative and smiled so much it scared me. We moved to a bigger apartment close to the city center, and once or twice a week, drove by the "magic" block of dazzling buildings. Even twelve years later I remained intensely curious, but now I wondered not only about the buildings, but the people inside. It must be movie stars and royalty going to dinner, having parties and dancing into the wee hours of the night. I would catch my mother looking at me out of the corner of her eye as I strained to get a good look through any window or opening door we passed.

I became brave enough to demand my mother tell me about my father. She went very quiet, wringing her hands and gazing up at the ceiling. As her face tilted down, she cleared her throat and said, "I am having a hard time finding the words that won't hurt you as much as they hurt me. Your father led a double life. He had another family. I was so blind to the clues. When he died, I was finally able to start over. The courts divided funds he had set aside for his children, and it helped me get training and a better job. I put the rest into a trust fund for you, and have paid back every penny that I borrowed."

I cried and hugged her very tightly. My story about top secret work wasn't so far off, after all. That night, I went to my room and tried to remember everything about my father as clearly as possible. I decided that I wanted to meet his other family someday, but not for a long time. Sleep was a lot of tossing and turning, and some very strange dreams.

When I woke, I remembered part of one, and my plan took form. I was going to the magic block with my mother. Every shop would be on our list. I would save every penny from my babysitting jobs and any other windfall that came my way.

Several months later the magical day arrived. I could hardly wait. Imagination and reality were about to collide. "Here we go!" was my shout as we got out of the car.

Heaven on Wheels

Ann Antognoli

People love heroes. We even lavish accolades on individuals who perform single acts of courage and transform them into instant celebrities. Occasionally, in the midst of all the hero madness, a person captures our imagination and shines for eternity.

While every town is blessed with its share of quiet heroes, the New Castle Area Transit Authority had no way of knowing that it was hiring one of them the day it hired Ernie Orelli. Ernie was an unassuming man applying for a less than glamorous job as a city bus driver. After getting hired, he liked to interact with passengers, especially the older ones whom he made feel welcome, comfortable, and safe.

Outwardly, Ernie seemed ordinary, but I'd catch a glimpse of his extraordinary character each time I visited my 92-year-old mother, Sarifa Abraham. The fact that my mother had four sons and two daughters who doted on her didn't stop her from doting on Ernie as though he were her fifth son. She told me stories of how Ernie would jump off the bus and sprint to *The Medicine Shoppe* to pick up her prescriptions each time she absent-mindedly forgot to stop on the way to catching his bus. My mother told me how he would lower the bus step to make boarding the bus a little easier for her. With appreciation, she would recall from time to time how he even changed a small section of the bus route near the Vista South Apartments where she lived to allow her and other senior companions easier and safer access to the bus, minimizing daily battles with dangerous traffic.

The unlikely bond between this young bus driver and my 92-year-old mother grew clearer the evening I overheard a phone call between Ernie and my mother. He called to remind her that he'd be on vacation for the week. After she wished him well, and hung up the phone, she informed me that she'd be taking the week off from the Senior Citizens Center because she was tired. When I volunteered to drive her to and from the Center, she stubbornly refused. She only wanted to ride the bus if Ernie was driving. That's how I learned that Ernie's schedule became my mother's schedule. I watched my strong-willed, independent mother grow more and more dependent on this young bus driver who afforded her safe and secure passage through a world that was growing more challenging beyond the confines of her apartment.

My mother's story was also extraordinary. She was an intelligent, high-spirited, attractive woman who was born in Lebanon, grew up in Cuba, and migrated to America when her handsome new husband suggested that they be adventurous in their life together. While she was always proud of her Lebanese heritage, she was just as determined to earn her American citizenship. She spoke four languages fluently and loved to socialize and play practical jokes on family and friends. After raising six children, she remained active all her life, but time took its toll during her 92 years, weakening her and slowing her down. With the aid of a walker, she began to move at a snail's pace. Her sight limited to one eye, she shrewdly began to avoid situations and activities where she would need to rely on others and grew keenly aware of the subtle ways society grudgingly tolerated the old among us. Mother found it increasingly difficult to relinquish her soaring spirit to the confines of a failing body.

It was natural that my mother and others like her gravitated toward a kind and generous spirit like Ernie Orelli. When he sensed their feelings of frustration as they boarded his bus to and from the Senior Citizens Center, he calmed them with his care. Despite their best efforts to catch a bus they feared would leave them behind, he cautioned them to move slowly, always waiting a little longer for them.

Ernie recognized the confusion that crossed my mother's face and the faces of her companions when they would board the wrong bus, so he'd gently guide them to the bus that would take them home. Rather than display indifference as they sat in silence, Ernie learned their names and engaged them with light-hearted discussions of family, friends, and food. That's why my mother felt at ease baking him loaves of Syrian bread and calling him at is home to ask if his cold was getting any better. He never failed to answer her with a jovial, "I'm okay, Mrs. Abraham. See you on the bus tomorrow." She'd hang up the phone with an air of confidence, anticipating that the new day would bring an expectation of joy.

We never told my mother that Ernie died too young. Ninety-two-year-olds should never bear that kind of heartbreak. Still, after the visits and phone calls stopped, she seemed to know.

Ernie Orelli's life was too short, but we thank him for helping those who lived so long. Although his inordinate stewardship for my mother and the senior citizens he encountered never made headlines, his life carried more meaning than earthly chronicles register.

When my mother died a year after Ernie Orelli, we knew that God sent him to meet her, to guide my mother safely home.

Originally published Nov 28, 2002, New Castle News.

Line Dancing

Dorothy Burchett Knight

Some people have lived in New Castle and surrounding area all of their lives. I'm a newcomer. By that, I mean I moved here six years ago, when I married my second husband. It wasn't easy to pick up from my roots and moved sixty miles away. I had lived in a rural area and this seemed to me to be much more urban. Of course, it isn't anything like Pittsburgh or New York City, or Chicago, and I wouldn't want it to be. As soon as I moved here, I knew I was going to like it.

There are all kinds of opportunities, if a person wants to take advantage of them. Of course, there will always be people who will disagree with that idea, but I've found it to be a lot of fun. Being a senior citizen, the first thing my husband did was to introduce me to Challenges, the senior center on Highland Avenue. That's where he would spend many of his mornings—drinking coffee, reading the newspaper and visiting with whomever sat at the table where he was sitting. It wasn't long before I found that Challenges was more than that.

For instance, lunch is available five days a week, except when closed for the holidays. There is an exercise class every day of the week, for those people who want to keep fit, as well as Yoga and Zumba. Some people prefer less active pursuits, such as knitting, card games and art class. Of course, no senior center would be complete without Bingo several times a week. Before each of the major holidays, the center holds a party—a hearty meal, door prizes and entertainment. Some people, who don't have their own transportation, go to Challenges on the New Castle Transit bus or the ACTS bus. It seems there is always a way to get there for those who want to go.

Although I tried exercise and Zumba, what really caught my eye was line dancing. I had never line danced before, but it looked like fun. I soon started falling in line with the other dancers and, although I made a lot of missteps, I kept on going. I went three times a week, at first. Then, one of the classes was dropped and I went twice a week. Speaking of

Challenges, I found it to be a challenge to learn all of the steps that were involved—not to mention the number of different dances. There are thousands! (I can remember a few.)

I started dancing in 2014, but the line dancing group has been in existence since 2002, when the center first opened. Some of the line dancers say they were waiting in line, outside the building, to sign up for Challenges (and line dancing) on the day it opened and they've been dancing ever since. The group was very welcoming. They were anxious to show me the steps and encourage me to keep coming. They were my first friends upon moving into the area.

I enjoy many things about line dancing. It's fun, it helps to keep me fit and I get to visit with people with the same interests. For senior citizens, who say there's nothing to do in New Castle, I recommend Challenges and, if you're adventurous, try line dancing.

The Legend of the Pumpkin Patch

Lavonne Lyles

I want to tell you about a Pumpkin Patch a long time ago.

Nobody cared about it so it decided not to grow.

Nobody really gave a hoot. Nobody cried.

As well as can be expected, that Pumpkin Patch died.

But to everyone's astonishment, to all who did not care,

That God forsaken Pumpkin Patch only died there.

It grew in every child's heart on the night of Halloween

It was on display at festivals where its goodness could be seen.

So, if you're ever overtaken when people just don't care,

Just think about the Pumpkin Patch, it's EVERYWHERE.

This poem was inspired by and is dedicated to the I-CARE House, a comprehensive community center and learning field site created to enhance the quality of life in a low-income neighborhood. It was located on Court Street and directed by Alice Kaiser-Drobney.

Bev Martinko

St. Mary's Church, N. Beaver Street, New Castle. Mary, Mother of Hope Catholic Church.

New Castle Man - Noted New York Artist

By Betty Hoover DiRlsio

David Harry Gaibis was born in Naples, Italy March 14, 1879. It was said he started his career at the age of nine studying in Italy and that he helped paint the noted Scala Di Milan Opera House in Milan, Italy. While in Naples, he completed a course of study at the Institute of Art. An artist, and decorator, he aided in the work of decorating the buildings in Paris for the World's Exposition in 1900.

He immigrated under the name of Davide Gaibisso to New York on December 3, 1901 aboard the *Sicily,* bringing with him his brother Eugene's daughter, Linda, who was 4 years of age at the time. The two were detained for about 48 hours and released into the custody of his sister-in-law Carmella De Santis Gaibis.

Coming to New Castle as early as 1907, he painted the frescoes at the Warner brothers' first theater in New Castle, the Cascade. By 1913 he was working for the Frew Furniture Company as a decorator. With mechanical abilities, he also patented a slot-ticketing machine for use in the new motion picture industry.

He completed 22 fine oil paintings that hung for sale in Emery Wall Paper Company on N. Mill St. using his own family as a model for a painting entitled "The First Baby". Another picture purportedly showed a group of newsboys in the street near the news office playing marbles. Several of the scenes were landscapes and ocean scenes.

By 1917 he owned a Mural Decorating Shop for interior and exterior decorations at 35 N. Mill. Gaibis was a painting foreman for the B&O Railroad in 1920. At one point, he was associated with T. W. Nelson Company and the Marshall Field Company of Chicago as its leading decorator, and with other concerns of Cleveland. In 1922 "Gaibis & Dercole" Interior Decorators opened up a new store as dealers in China and Glassware at 13 E. Long Ave. By 1924 he was working for New Castle Paint & Glass Co., 107 E. North St., as an interior decorator.

He later found work in New York and for ten years he commuted by train to New York City, returning home on weekends. In New York, he was affiliated with Rambusch Decorating Company, a well-known firm. He helped decorate the interior of the Empire State Building, being one of the supervisors and artists decorating the lobby and observation room. He also was in charge of decorating the huge Roxy Theatre in New York. Gaibis was employed by Brounet Studios, another noted firm, and while there painted the interior of the palatial residence of Anthony Compagna, Riverdale, NY. While in Brooklyn he painted the interior of the Paramount Theater.

After ten years he returned to New Castle. Locally he directed the painting of the art work in the interior of the Benjamin Franklin, Jr. High Auditorium, the old Coliseum theatre, New Castle Hospital, St. Vitus Church and a number of other places including the old YMCA, YWCA and many of the fine older homes in the city.

Prior to his death on May 5, 1936, he was working for the Works Progress Administration Artists Project, in New Castle. PHOTO: Betty Hoover DiRisio (Copyright 2015)

David Gaibis, courtesy of Stephanie Fulena, granddaughter of David Gaibis.

Hell-View Manor

Randy Ryan

The first thought that ran through Zach's head as he browsed Hill View Manor's website on his laptop was, *this couldn't be more perfect.* The ambient lighting of the classically designed website reflected in his glasses, which began to slide down his nose. He pushed them up and continued reading. Growing up in the New Castle area, he'd heard the tales, but they were always nothing more than hearsay. Now, he had a source of information that was, at the very least, semi-credible. Nothing could be more befitting of an amateur ghost hunter's first expedition.

His cellphone screen lit up, casting an added aura of blue glow in the darkness of his apartment. Zach looked at the screen and saw the name Stan glowering at him. With a swipe of his finger, he slid the bobbing icon to the right. He pressed the green accept button.

"Hello."

"Are you making any headway?" Stan said.

"You're going to love this," Zach said. "Hill View Manor. I remember about fifteen years ago, just after it closed, that show *Ghost Hunters* conducted a search there. From what I've been reading, the activity hasn't died down any since its abandonment. It's perfect."

"Well," Stan said, "I suppose it can't be any worse than the Hoyt Institution. You remember, that place we did back in Willow Falls?"

"Yeah, I remember," Zach said. "That was around Christmastime. Those two thieves—Hanson and Cutter, I think their names were— robbed the place before plowing into the back of a damn police cruiser."

Zach pushed his glasses up. "Have you ever read anything about the history of Hill View? It's pretty rich. This could be great for us."

"Well I'm down," Stan said. "Who do we go about contacting?"

"It says on their website they have staff and volunteers working regularly, and armed officers routinely patrol the grounds. After the Discovery Channel went there, the place became a huge hotspot. I imagine all we have to do is call or show up and ask to speak to a warden on one of the floors. I'm sure they'd love to have us."

Stan cleared his throat. "Let's stop by tomorrow morning, get a feel for the place."

"Tomorrow morning it is. I'll pick you up bright and early."

Zach loved driving through Shenango Township. It was one of many townships surrounding the New Castle area, including Ellwood, which was just north of Shenango. There was a Subway, Big Lots, Family Dollar, Goodwill and the plaza which housed K-Mart, Great Wall, Dollar Tree, Hallmark and T & M Hardware. Of course, there was Shenango Area School District, Zach's alma matter. He smiled as they passed, recalling fond memories. His gut tingled as they came to the Dairy Queen up the hill. They were getting excitingly close.

"It'll be up ahead on the left," he said.

"You know," Stan said. "We may have to stop and grab ourselves a cone from Forbush's. They close for the season in September, so we only have a couple more weeks. A butter peakon or black raspberry sounds like heaven."

"Business before pleasure," Zach said. "I called and spoke to a lady on the phone. They know we're coming."

"What's the game plan?"

"Same as everybody else's," Zach said. "Talk to historians and witnesses, walk around the courtyard and building, get to know the lay of the land. That kind of thing."

He steered onto a side road surrounded by nothing but small fields and woods. The greenery of the trees and grass provided a strong, contrast to the pure blue sky. *The last remnants of summer are always the strongest*, Zach thought.

They came to a long driveway strewn with rocks. It led directly to the ominous structure. Despite its harrowing presence, replete with old slabs of stone the color of fresh concrete and small windows, heavily barred, A flutter of excitement tore through Zach's stomach. He seconded every one of Stan's notions. The peaked roofs and angular architecture, including gargoyles, probably carved of granite and perched on ledges, put the final touches on it. To a ghost hunter, the scarier the better.

"There's no way we're going to turn up empty," Stan said. "Just look at this place. I haven't seen it in so long, I almost forgot what it looked like in person."

They pulled up the driveway to base of a grassy hill supporting the old mental hospital. Zach got out, stretching his arms and legs, without taking his eyes off the building towering over them. It blocked the sun and cast a shadow as dark as gloom.

A distinguished voice startled Zach. "Good afternoon." The words carried a thick German accent. "I have been awaiting your arrival."

An older gentleman wearing a white lab coat approached. Zach thought he looked like a mad scientist, with his checkered undershirt and wavy silver hair. A pair of dark eyes glared madly from a face that seemed to consist entirely of a prominently pointed nose and overly-long moustache.

"I'm Doctor Ernst Greenway." He extended his hand. Zach took it delicately.

"So nice to meet you," he said, feigning a smile. Something about the old man seemed wrong, something he couldn't put his finger on. Although, to be fair, he'd only known the man for approximately two seconds. "I believe we spoke on the phone."

"Indeed," Dr. Greenway said. He nodded toward Stan. "Who is your friend?"

"This is Stan. We do all of our investigations together."

Stan extended his hand. "It's a pleasure," he said.

"The pleasure is all mine," Dr. Greenway said sincerely. "So, I understand that I'm to give you the grand tour before you set up for the night."

"If it wouldn't be too much trouble," Zach said. "We're technically considered amateurs. The difference between an amateur and a professional is that professionals get paid for what they do. We're hoping we can shed some light on a few things here. Maybe someday we can do this for a living."

"It is no trouble at all," Greenway said. "Everybody has to start somewhere. I will lead if you can stick closely behind. It is easy to lose one's way in this place, certainly."

Greenway turned and strode into the shadows. Zach and Stan followed. Greenway pulled a round keychain from of his pocket. Gold and bronze keys jangled in a breeze that picked up at just that moment.

Weird, Zach thought.

Greenway inserted a key into an invisible lock. It was too dark to see details. Zach shivered. Why was this door locked? It wasn't as if there were patients left to look after. But, if that was the case, why was this guy dressed like a doctor?

You're not even inside and you're losing it. Maybe he's conducting research and wants to look the part. The thought didn't comfort Zach. Had Greenway walked out this door, closed and locked it without them noticing? Or, had he been waiting out here the whole time they were driving up? Either way it wasn't normal.

Inside, the temperature plummeted. Zach gasped and stopped in his tracks. Going from the warmth of the late-August sun to the sudden chill of the long dark hallway was shocking. Greenway closed and locked the door behind them. The click of the bolt seemed to echo from everywhere at once.

Zach blinked. His eyes needed a moment to adjust. Going from the piercing brightness to this darkness and dinge was as much of a shock as going from hot to cold.

"Man, I'm getting some really interesting vibes here," Stan said, rubbing his arms with his opposite hands. "What's the story behind this place?" he asked Greenway. "I'm familiar with it as a location, but my knowledge regarding its actual history is, I guess, a little superficial."

"Such is the case with everybody who hasn't actually stepped foot inside," Greenway said. "The truth is, the history here is rather troubled. The two of you are attracted to such things, no?"

"Have you talked to many people on the subject?" Zach said.

"I have given a number of tours," Greenway said. "In this area, as you may already be aware, historical landmarks are an attraction."

A noise penetrated the stone wall. It sounded like a muffled scream.

"Did you hear that?" Zach said.

"Uh, yeah?" Stand said. He sounded startled.

"Hillview Manor opened its doors on October 31st, 1926," Greenway said. Zach glanced at Stan's shadowy form. There was no way Greenway hadn't heard their exchange or that sound.

"It was known as Lawrence County's Home for the Aged," Greenway continued, "but more derogatory connotations labeled it as the poor house or poor farm, as it housed all of the areas mentally ill, severely destitute and elderly residents without known family." He continued walking like a man on a mission.

They passed old cells and rooms guarded by heavily reinforced, bolted doors. He must be used to it all, but Zach couldn't help but take in every detail in the sporadic, stark lighting. *You'd think they'd hire an electrician, considering that people still worked here.*

"When it first opened," Greenway said, "it was run by Perry and Mary Snyder along with their two children and twelve staff members. Initially, it housed twenty inmates. By June of 1944, Mr. Snyder and his wife, who were both seventy-nine years of age, were accused, quite unconvincingly by the way, of incompetency. This led to a hearing. They won their pensions but were forced to retire. They were given three weeks to vacate the premises."

Zach tested his voice. "In 1969 it was remodeled and turned into a skilled nursing center, right?"

"That is correct," Greenway said. "Where I am taking you now is an area known as the North Wing, but we like to call it the Green Wing.

You will see why in a moment, a renovation undertaken during Christmastime in 1975."

Greenway retrieved his jangling keys. The door he was unlocked was so thick and oblong that it resembled a bank vault. Zach exchanged glances with Stan.

Once Greenway opened the door completely, he understood why it was called the Green Wing. Everything in sight—walls, ceiling, floor—was colored the greenest shade of green, almost headache-inducing. Lighting came from two incandescent bulbs fixed to the ceiling.

Zach wondered whether this was a psychological strategy from more archaic science, a tactic to keep hyperactive lunatics in place. He didn't bother to ask.

"In addition to what you see here," Greenway said, "a three-story extension and alternate basement floor were built. Ultimately, the facility was renamed Hillview Manor not long after, in June of 1977. It closed its doors in 2004 due to financial constraints." He continued straight ahead, leading them down the green north wing.

Where is he taking us? "Let's talk a little about the supposed hauntings," Zach said. "I read on your website that over one-hundred people throughout the years have reported unnatural activity, typically during the night. Have you experienced anything personally?"

Greenway opened a door at the end of the hallway. It led to a set of metal, mesh stairs. "This will take us onto the roof. I want to give you boys a proper view of the courtyard."

The roof was a big and open space. Greenway took a deep breath through his nose. It sounded exaggerated, and Zach was certain he saw the man's eyes roll back as if he were inhaling some sublime aroma and wanted to concentrate on just that. "We are closer to God," he whispered under his breath.

We weren't meant to hear that, Zach thought. He made eye-contact with Stan. *What in the world did that mean?*

Greenway led them to a ledge. "As you can see, our courtyard is still very open. Years ago, patients were free to wander, supervised, of course, within its boundaries."

Zach thought of Stonehenge. There was an area for tables in the shape of a circle with rocks serving as the linoleum. The tables were also round and looked to be carved from stone. Sacrificial altars? The stone were be old and weathered, probably because the courtyard had been vacant for so long. Grass surrounded the seating area, but it was barricaded by a tall, black iron fence upon which somebody could easily be impaled.

"To elaborate upon your question," Greenway said, "I personally have not experienced anything paranormal, or supernatural, if you like that term better. However, I have a file in my office detailing numerous firsthand accounts about the experiences that you two are seeking. Many are fairly recent."

"We'd love to see them," Stan said. Zach nodded. Recently active places were naturally the best to stake out for a thorough investigation.

"These reports are typical amongst your demographic," Greenway said with a slight nod. "For lack of a better term. Unexplained noises and voices, sightings of apparitions, objects moved, windows opened and closed without any rational cause, extreme shifts in temperature. All of it is there."

Zach grinned. This place had a little of everything going for it.

Greenway raised a finger as if suddenly recalling an important thought. "Earlier in the summer, a cable technician was doing an install. He was running a line through the basement when approached by a gentleman in casual attire who he assumed was an employee. They carried on a full conversation, and when he went upstairs to get tools from his truck, he encountered one of the cooks. He asked who the gentleman was. She told him there was nobody down there besides himself. The only way into that sector was through the kitchen, and he was the only one who'd come or gone all morning. The incident left him so startled that he left the job unfinished and abandoned whatever equipment he had brought in."

Excitement conquered dread. "This sounds perfect, Dr. Greenway," Zach said. "Stan and I would love to set up our equipment for the night. Maybe we can shed some light on this place. We didn't bring a medium with us, but we do have the machinery to capture EVP's—that's electronic voice phenomena—or voices generally considered to come from the spirit world that cannot be heard on the regular spectrum."

"I do not see why that would be a problem," Greenway said. "But first, allow me to show you the rest of the building."

They followed him back inside. Zach shot one last glance at the beating sun descending from its zenith. Soon, there would be no light.

Night had fallen. The temperature outside had cooled off, but Zach didn't notice a considerable change in the building. He and Stan had their headphones, amplifier, recording devices and night vision cameras set up. Greenway had gone for the evening and there was nobody working the graveyard shift. With the silence and just the two of them, everything was perfect.

"Boy, Dr. Greenway is quite a character, huh?" Stan said.

"He sure is," Zach said. "There's something a little off about him. He kind of weirded me out."

"Me too. And we're paranormal investigators. What was that comment he made up on the roof?"

"The one about being closer to God? That was a little bit disturbing, wasn't it? Maybe it's a good thing, though, because we might strike gold."

They walked down abandoned corridors, unable to see more than two or three feet in front of their faces. The walls groaned, the building settled into its foundation, but otherwise, nothing exciting. Nevertheless, the night was young.

"Is there anybody with us?" Zach said, holding out his parabolic microphone. "If you are here, give us a sign. Speak your name, say the date you were born and died."

Nothing, no response, at least not within the normal range of human hearing. Just as Zach was beginning to appreciate how quiet it was, a sound issued forth, a repetitive, echoing whisper, something like *Sa, Sa, Sa.*

"Do you hear that?" Stan asked excitedly.

"Yeah, listen." The noise pierced the darkness again. *Sa, Sa, Sa.*

"It's coming from the end of this corridor," Zach said. The hallway was long and dark, giving off the illusion of endlessness and eternally-blackness. Zach felt as if he was peering into the psyche of a demented serial killer.

"I think we're in the Green Wing," Stan said.

"Where's the light switch?" Zach said. The darkness was suddenly too much. Stan laughed nervously. They proceeded toward the end of the hall, but no matter how close they got, the sound still sounded far off.

They reached the door to the roof. Zach touched the knob.

The noise ceased.

Stan tapped Zach's shoulder repeatedly. "We captured something, buddy! We got it!" He pointed to the earphone pressed to his ear.

"Really?" Zach laughed. "Wow."

Zach barely noticed their return to the atrium where they'd set up headquarters. It was much easier to see here because the atrium was made entirely of glass, and the full moon flooded the area with chalky light.

Zach hooked Stan's recorder to the machine he used to translate subharmonic, infrasonic and ultrasonic transmissions. A mechanical buzz quickly became a nerve-wracking hum. *We may have hit the lottery on this one*, he thought.

Rather than revealing the repetitive hissing in greater clarity, something quite different came through. The line that traced across the screen like a heart monitor spiked. A shrill voice became audible, hitting frequencies that Zach had never seen. *Most certainly inhuman.*

"We are closer to God," the demonic voice said.

This was what they came for, but Zach suddenly wondered if they hadn't bitten off a little more than their jaws could handle. This wasn't a response to one of Stan's questions, or even random jibber; it was what Greenway had whispered, word for word. The phrase repeated with even more fervor. Zach stepped back. Stan knocked a radios onto the floor, causing it to shatter.

"All of a sudden, I'm not liking this so much," Zach said.

Stan pounded the table. His throat corded, teeth clenched..

"Stan? Are you all right?"

"Jesus Christ, stop it," Stan cried out. "Goddam it, I'm burning up, I'm burning up!" He laughed an insane, lunatic sound, and began tearing his shirt.

Zach reached out. Stan swatted his hand away. Zach had told Stan many tales about ghost hunters being overtaken, or *possessed*. He feared that could be happening to his friend now.

Stan quieted. He leveled his eyes on Zach. "You want to know the truth?" he said. His glare became a gaze leveled on Zach.

"Yes," Zach said calmly, "I do." What should he do to help his buddy? Was 9-1-1 an option? He hadn't tested his phone for reception.

Stan laughed, voice shrilling until it was no longer his. His eyes ignited into coals of blue-white fire. Zach wanted to run, but his legs would not cooperate.

When Stan spoke again, he had a heavy European accent, a *German* accent. "The Nazis had agents stationed here in Western Pennsylvania. Our studies were classified above top secret. We were able to open up a gateway, a portal to a dimension of pure chaos, pure *evil*."

Greenway, Zach thought frantically.

Stan took a plodding step. Zach edged back. He bumped into something, startling him further. Equipment scattered and crashed.

"We tore a hole in the fabric, Zach. We *saw* the unadulterated horror that exists on the other side." Stan sniffed. "Exposure to insanity is enough to drive a man to suicide, if it does not kill him outright. But we *harnessed* the power. This location, this place. *Here*. We were able to contain it, control it."

Zach swallowed thickly. "Stan? Buddy?" Stan's eyes turned a hateful red. The full moon went bloody, painting the atrium with ensanguined light.

"After the war," the Stan-thing said, "surviving agents went into hiding. We brought our secrets with us, and now, it is time to show you the truth. We discovered the secret. We became eldritch." Laser beams shot from Stan's eyes, searing Zach's retinas, drilling through his optic nerves, burning into his brain.

A human scream rang. Vivid images filled Zach's head, depraved men with monstrous helmets and suits adorned with blood metals. Understanding dawned. He was part of a history that persisted to this day. There were never any spirits. There were only things far worse.

A haunter shambled forth. Zach thought of one word: *Unspeakable*.

Mahoningtown

Robert Stull

In a small city, with two traffic lights
You could walk from end to end,
Windows wide open, doors never locked
We were among all our family and friends.

Growing up in this town with little to fear
We always had something to do,
Out until dark and sometimes beyond
But our parents did know who was who.

We also had a movie theater
And little 'Mom and Pop' stores,
A pizza shop, where smell of the sauce
Would draw you right into their door.

We mustn't forget, setting up pins
At the bowling alley by the bridge,
For some of us, it was our first job
But seemed more like a privilege.

We had churches and restaurants
And a hotel... with a history of its own,
We had our own Post Office, even a bank
And a train station to go town to town.

MAHONINGTOWN 56

There were many other establishments
Where the hard workin' men would go,
To relax and unwind after a day
In steel mills, factories or rail roads.

The rumble of trains, day and night
This town, they would pass through,
It did not seem to bother too many
It was a part of life we all knew.

In the summer we had, many street fairs
Where it seemed the whole town would meet,
The bands and the music and the parades
And all would march to their beat.

The bakery, a library and even a school
Shoe stores and barber shops,
Hardware and groceries, always at hand
And a gunsmith in his little gun shop.

Playgrounds all within walking distance
With slides, swings, a merry go round,
Gas stations, newsstand, a laundromat
A park full of trees, shaded the grounds.

The ball fields, the gift shop and custard stand
It's in our memories, those we will keep,
It was once a very prospering place
Our own village, that didn't sleep.

57 ROBERT STULL

Yes, In a small city, with two traffic lights

It seemed you could forever roam,

Windows wide open, doors never locked

Mahoningtown, the place we call "Home!'

O Tempo

(the weather, the time in Portuguese)

Rich Yates

The Beginning

I have always been interested in the weather, especially from high school on. Early on my interest was in generalized science—specifically Geology and Paleontology. Then something clicked. Maybe it was the winter—that most interested me. Like the days off from school. There was a big snow in the 50's at my childhood home of Titusville, NJ. I remember hitting my teeth on a sapling while sledding in the "Little Woods." I remember the effects of rain and strong wind in Hurricane Hazel in 1954. I have always been awed by the power of the weather in fierce thunderstorms. I have yet to see that most violent weather experience—a tornado.

My junior high school years were spent in Maryville, Tennessee. Science in general continued to interest me. By high school at Morrisville, PA I had narrowed down my scientific interest to meteorology. I ordered a copy of the weekly publication of daily weather maps from the National Weather Bureau. I paid attention to the weather forecasts and the weather maps published in the newspaper. I decided to study to become a meteorologist. My parents got me a barometer which helped me detect changes in the weather in advance.

Early College

I was accepted to Maryville College, Maryville, Tennessee, to start the fall of 1964. I was familiar with the campus, as I had lived in Maryville with my family while my dad studied at Maryville College from 1957-1961. Maryville College is a small liberal arts Presbyterian related college nestled near the foothills of the Great Smoky Mountains. My plan was to major in math then transfer to Penn State in my junior year and begin study of meteorology.

While at Maryville one meteorological incident stuck out in my mind. Once in winter it went down to -10 degrees Fahrenheit after a 10-inch snowstorm. Typically; however, snow did not last long in Maryville. In the Smoky Mountains it could be a different story. During my earlier stint in Maryville I remember making a Boy Scout hike in the late 1950's in 6-inch snow. We hiked to our overnight camp in a log cabin. Once again, I digressed.

The Transfer that Wasn't

My sophomore year I was accepted to transfer to Penn State to study meteorology. My dream of becoming a meteorologist looked like it could come true. But I managed only C's in my major—Math—at Maryville. I would bother the smarter math majors at their bedtime to help me with my homework in calculus. I managed a B in Physics the first semester of my sophomore year but crashed on electronics in the second semester. The result was a D. This and my shyness and not wanting to lose the familiarity of little Maryville College caused me to decide not to transfer. I changed my major to Psychology. I was able to handle this major independently.

Senior Year Decisions

My senior year was 1968. The Viet Nam War was on. I was to be drafted upon graduation. I decided to enlist in the U.S. Army to have a better chance of not being sent to Viet Nam. Also I was able to choose my U.S. Army advanced training school. I chose a 19-week Meteorological Observation course. I enlisted in the U.S. Army shortly after my graduation from Maryville College in June of 1968.

U.S. Army

Ft. Campbell, KY

My basic training was in Ft. Campbell, KY. I had to work hard to pass the physical proficiency tests especially in the strength areas. But I persevered and received orders to report to Ft. Monmouth, NJ after my leave. Meteorological Observation training was to begin.

Ft. Monmouth, NJ

After basic training at Ft. Campbell, KY in 1968, I started Meteorological Observer training at Ft. Monmouth, NJ. There were three components of the 19-week course: Surface Observations, Micromet, and Upper Air. What interested me most were surface operations and upper air. Surface observations included recording of air temperature, dew points, relative humidity, barometric pressure, cloud types, cloud cover, precipitation, and surface winds. Upper air included inflating helium balloons, attaching radiosondes, orienting tracking equipment to the radiosonde, releasing the balloon, using the GMD tracker to pick up radiosonde signals, recording the results of the signals on graphs which showed temperature change with height, upper air winds, and upper air barometric pressure. This data could be used for weather forecasts and helping with meteorological weather rocket shots. I did very well in the course and graduated in April of 1969. After a month of leave and meeting my Brazilian wife to be I left for my "overseas" duty at Ft. Greely, Alaska.

Ft. Greely, AK

I married my Brazilian pen pal at Ft. Greely. She flew up from Charleston, SC to marry me. In Alaska I was part of USA Met Team Alaska, sending up weather balloons for weather forecasts and support for weather rocket shots.

Fall of 1969 came quickly—the aspen leaves turned yellow and fell. Winter arrived. One time the crew except me had been out late partying and didn't show for the early morning weather balloon release. My wife and I performed the basic release functions alone. My wife held and released the balloon and radiosonde while I oriented the GMD signal tracking device to the radiosonde's signals. The data were plotted later when the crew finally arrived. On the release log I recorded in Portuguese "So um"—only one (of the crew).

We had some -40 F/-40C weather that winter, but not as much as was hoped, as this was the arctic test site for weapons. At -30 F tires of cars froze on the bottom, and cars limped along when started until the tires warmed up. Of course, cars had engine block and battery warmers and antifreeze circulators.

I rose to the rank of E-5, and I also studied for and received proficiency pay in my MOS 93E20--Meteorological Observer. Most one-termers didn't bother with this, but every little bit of extra money helped as my wife soon became pregnant and had a very nauseous pregnancy.

It was an 18-month tour of duty at Ft. Greely. Close to my time of transfer back to Ft. Monmouth in October of 1970 it turned winter quickly. We even had 6 inches of snow on the ground on Labor Day 1970.

Ft. Monmouth Again

I completed my active duty time at Ft. Monmouth, NJ in the winter and spring of 1970 and 1971. My daughter, Natalie, was born at Patterson Army Hospital at Ft. Monmouth on December 29, 1970.

At Ft. Monmouth I worked in surface observations. Surface observations included air temperature, dew point, relative humidity, barometric pressure, surface winds, cloud type and cover, and precipitation. It was an official weather observation point. It was a typical winter and spring for New Jersey. One time the temperature got down to 2 F. I was honorably discharged from the U.S. Army on June 21, 1971.

A Little about My Nature

My nature has been a lot like the weather—very changeable. In later years I have appeared to calm down some.

What to Do after the Army?

This question presented itself. I thought about studying for the Presbyterian ministry, but my wife was against that. Once again, I applied for the Peace Corps, but I wasn't accepted. This was really a good thing, as I now had a family.

I heard an advertisement for the Teacher Corps, a government program that had prospective teachers complete a master's degree in teaching at a university, teach, and do community work

East Tennessee State University

A Teacher Corps program existed at East Tennessee State University in Johnson City, Tennessee. I went alone and tried out the program for two weeks. I decided to stay the course. My wife, daughter, and I began our life in Johnson City, Tennessee. We lived in an apartment on Narrow Lane.

I started the course July of 1971 and graduated June of 1973. Details of this time may be expounded upon later. I do remember making an instructional video of presenting a weather forecast. So, weather continued to be on my mind.

Rio de Janeiro

The Preparation to Leave

My wife missed life and family in Brazil and left for Brazil in May 1973 before I graduated from ETSU. I graduated and spent a short time at my parents' house in Union, PA. I picked up work as a meat processing plant manager at a motel chain in Lancaster, PA. But I was preparing to be reunited with my wife and daughter in Rio de Janeiro, Brazil. I obtained a Brazilian permanent visa (this involved some trips to the Brazilian Consulate in New York City) and left for Brazil in August of 1973.

Rio Teaching

I was planning to work for an English course, but when I arrived that position had already been taken. I applied and was hired as an elementary school teacher at the American School of Rio de Janeiro, Brazil. I taught third grade four and a half years and fifth grade three and a half years. The last year there I taught at Our Lady of Mercy School as an E.S.L. Teacher. My total teaching experience in Rio spanned the years 1973-1982. More expansion on this time will be forthcoming in future writing.

Weather in Rio and Brazil

My interest in weather continued. I went to the Rio airport— Galeao—once to talk to meteorologists there.

I was interested in low temperatures as always. The lowest it got where I lived in Rio de Janeiro was 52 F. Rio has a near tropical climate. It is about the latitude of Havana, Cuba in the northern hemisphere. Winters are cooler; sometimes the highs may be in the 60's and lows in the upper 50's. But intervals of warm weather in the 80's by day are common even in winter. Summer has relatively constant heat with highs in the 80's to over 100 F and lows in the 70's. Rainfall is similar to places in the eastern U.S.

In the south of Brazil, it occasionally snows in winter, but it doesn't last.

Return to the U.S.

In June–August 1982 I was splitting up with my wife. I returned to the U.S. in August of 1982. I left my wife and two children in Rio. I was legally separated in Brazil. In 1985 I obtained a U.S. divorce. My weather interest became passive. Thankfully my first winter back wasn't very cold. I think it might have gotten down to 12 F a few times. This was at my parents' house in Claysville, PA, in the southwestern part of the state. Much of my time spent in Washington County has been written about earlier, especially in my first book: *A Love Book*.

Time Passes

I ended up in New Castle, PA in 1993. There was a big snow in March 1993; it snowed 36 inches. I was young and able to shovel my mother's driveway out.

I got work teaching adult literacy at a local adult education agency. My active interest in interest was rekindled. I worked up and presented a supplementary weather unit with materials from the National Weather Service.

Current Day

My interest in weather continues. My traditional teaching nowadays is limited to volunteering to teach a U.S. History class for about 15-20 minutes twice a month at a mental health outreach facility.

But my study of weather continues. I recommend a textbook by Lutgens and Tarbuck entitled, *The Atmosphere*. It is a great basic meteorology course that is updated every two years. Nowadays with apps on phones many have a chance to see weather forecasts instantaneously. Despite much larger computing power meteorology remains an inexact science. It is able to forecast general ideas relatively well but not the exact specifics.

Cold weather, and extreme heat are now difficult for me. As of this writing I am 72 years old. I'm out in the weather a lot in my rudimentary capacity as a gas pumper at a local full-service gas station. I try to dress appropriately, but my hands invariably get cracked in the cold.

I do, however, believe in climate change with accompanying warming of our planet Earth. I believe examination of facts leads to the conclusion that manmade emissions are causing much of the current warming. It needs to be pointed out continually the difference between weather (the atmospheric conditions of a locale at one specific time) and climate (a cumulative study of the weather at a specific locale over a period of many years). For additional information please, please look up statements by the American Meteorological Society on climate change and its causes.

Bibliographical Notes

"Climate Change: An Information Statement of the American Meteorological Society" (Adopted by the AMS Council 20 August 2012).

Frederick K. Lutgens and Edward J. Tarbuck: *The Atmosphere: An Introduction to Meteorology* (Glenview, IL: Pearson Education, Inc., 2013).

An Invitation to Believe

Marcelle Neumann

It began with an invitation. The medium asked permission to enter my personal space. Having experienced similar encounters, I had no qualms about allowing her to place her hands on my shoulders. I listened with an open mind as she gave me a message from my grandmother who had passed at the tender age of 93. I never freely discussed my beliefs with my grandmother unless she brought them up. My grandmother wanted me to know she was not in a place she expected, but she was none the less content. Although not some profound revelation, I accepted this as truth.

Some of my experiences over the years kept me searching for more answers. Others fed my soul in such a way I knew life would never be the same. My journey took me to places most would have thought fantastical. Native American medicine wheel ceremonies, visits to sacred sites, experiences with spiritual labyrinths, and even otherworldly encounters are part of what I encountered.

My decision to attend The Spiritual Path Church in New Castle, Pennsylvania was made with a curious mind. Since an early age, I believed there was more to life than what our basic senses could detect. I searched for what lies beyond the temporal world. Blessed with a parent whose beliefs mirrored mine, one Sunday we investigated New Castle's spiritualist church.

Often, we hear those who call themselves spiritual rather than religious. We all are inherently spiritual. Each one of us has the adeptness to acquire an empowered mind. Religions, however, bind one to a single thought. They have the belief that only one specific path is the right one to lead them to their destination. Being spiritual means having the self-reliance to travel your own way to the very same goal. Even in the terminology, one can ascertain the actual difference between the two. To follow a specific religion denotes one accepts its beliefs as the truth and therefore will not detour from that path. With spiritual individual, their inner essence is at a state of being or aspiring to be, at a level of divine consciousness. An individual who is, for example, a devout Catholic can, of course, be deeply spiritual as well.

The belief that the spirits of the dead can be contacted and pass on knowledge of an afterlife is at the core of spiritualism. Both spiritualism and spirituality have a connection with the idea of existence beyond human consciousness. Spirituality is not a product of religion. The process of transforming oneself from one state of mind to another has been identified by many faiths and interpreted in different ways.

I have been to several churches of different faiths. What I learned did not surprise me. There is a common desire within all. To know, not just believe, who we are, where we come from, and our individual purpose is what drives each of us to seek the truth. We may never obtain ultimate satisfaction in our search in one lifetime. However, each of us, no matter what path we take, seek the same goal.

As a child, I never had an interest in religion. My mother in her search to find a place to belong took my siblings and myself to the Unity Church. Founded in 1889 by Charles and Myrtle Fillmore, Unity is a Christian based church teaching a way of life which leads to happiness, health, prosperity, and peace. I grew up with this as my spiritual base and used it to travel other paths of enlightenment. My goal is a solid foundation to rest on in times of strife and as a steppingstone to other avenues taking me to a universal truth.

As I evolved, I gained a hunger for more spiritual based influences. I longed for new ways to invite joy and prosperity into my life. Each unique experience opened a new door. From Unity's knowledge, I ventured out to expand my mind and enrich my soul. The way I chose brought me to a small, unassuming building standing in a rural area of New Castle Pennsylvania. Regardless of denomination or belief, all are welcome. Affiliated with the Spiritualist's National Union of the United Kingdom, the New Castle church follows seven principles of truth.

Principle 1: Fatherhood of God

Spiritualists recognize there is a creative force in the universe. Many call this creative force "God." Much like a father is responsible for the origin or cause of our existence, the main principle of the spiritualist is acknowledging that this force manifests in all things. Knowing we are part of the life created by God, a spiritualist believes he is our Father.

Principle 2: Brotherhood of Man

Because we all come from the same universal Life source, we are, in effect, one large family. All humankind is part of a brotherhood. A brotherhood is a community sharing a common bond. As members of the same divine family, the connection we have precludes we must all work together to achieve the best for humanity.

Principle 3: The Communion of Spirits and the Ministry of Angels

While most religions believe in life after death, the spiritualist believes in the possibility of communication with departed spirits. Anyone can receive messages from beyond.

Principle 4: The Continuous Existence of the Human Soul

Spiritualist believe at the end of our present existence the human soul continues in a different form. We are created with energy or God Force, and when the current form has reached the end of its viability, it changes its manifestation. Science continues to confirm energy cannot be created nor destroyed. It is the very substance of which all are made and simply changes form. It will continue to create not from nothing but of itself. Believing the soul or spirit to be energy it is indestructible. On the death of the physical body, the spirit continues in a different form.

Principle 5: Personal Responsibility

This Principle is the one which places responsibility for wrongful thoughts and deeds where it belongs, with the individual. It is the acceptance of responsibility for every aspect of our lives and for what purpose we live our lives. No outside influences can interfere with any aspect of our development unless we are willing to allow this. Freewill makes our words, deeds, and thoughts our responsibility.

Principle 6: Compensation and Retribution Hereafter for all the Good and Evil deeds done on Earth

The natural or universal law of cause and effect is at the heart of the sixth principle of spiritualism. What is put forth in word, deed or action by an individual comes back as the same. The retributive effects of this law have a substantial impact on one's life and do not wait until that person passes over into the hereafter.

Principle 7: Eternal Progress Open to every Human Soul

There exists within most the desire to obtain a level of pure love and understanding. All human souls have the power to follow a progressive path that leads back to the GOD source, back to the origin of our existence.

Defined as the primary truth which serves as the foundation for a system of belief, these principles are found in many religions and faiths. During my journey, I came to realize the fundamental connection all these belief systems possessed. The messages I received at the spiritualist church in New Castle Pennsylvania served as a confirmation to my truth. With an open and eager mind, I followed my desire. While I sat in one of the chairs placed in front of the pulpit a member of the congregation approached me. She claimed to have the ability to contact the dead.

Attempts to communicate with the dead and other spirits have been documented back to early human history. In ancient times in the village of Endor, a woman lived who claimed to be a necromancer. She was said to be able to summon the spirits of the dead. In rebellion against God Saul, the current King of Israel sought out the witch. The armies of Israel were about to be attacked, and Saul was desperate. Interpretations of the story differ within various religions. Spiritualists have taken the story as evidence of mediumship. The medium has the role of an intermediary between the world of the living and the world of spirit. The Witch of Endor tells Saul he will perish in battle and as prophesied the army is defeated. Saul is fatally wounded and is said to have taken his own life.

We must not dismiss someone's beliefs as contrary as we follow our own path. If you are ever invited to attend the Spiritual Path Church in New Castle, Pennsylvania, do take the opportunity. In a calm and loving space, you will listen to an inspiring sermon. You may be blessed with a healing while someone lays their hands on your body. And if you desire to accept the invitation, it is possible you may receive a message from the spirit world. You just need to believe.

Music in Heaven

Lavonne Lyles

Will there be music in heaven, that man cannot take away
Or will the music in heaven be only for a day?

Will I have to leave this life, to bring back that sacred tune?
Then take me Jesus, take me, to the place where flowers bloom.

I long to hear the music that once filled my raptured soul.
I'll listen to the music, as the time begins to roll.

Eternity forever, and not just for a day.
The music up in heaven, man can never take away.

(inspired by the church choirs of New Castle)

The Voice of Angels

Lavonne Lyles

You sing with the voice of angels, and you play the organ fine.

But that heavenly voice of angels is with me all the time.

I hear it in the morning when the birds sing in the trees.

I hear it in the ocean waves, in a gentle summer breeze

How I love that sweet anointing that sets the captive free!

Oh, blessed voice of angels, sing another song for me!

(inspired by the church choirs of New Castle)

What I Fed My Brother

Colleen Seegers

When you grow up in a small town like New Castle and you have a vivid imagination, you start to do things you think will impress your parents. I was always busy at a young age thinking up deeds that would make them burst with pride.

I was four when my baby brother arrived. He wasn't too interesting until he started to crawl. He loved my attention. I was the best big sister. One Sunday morning my parents were upstairs getting ready for church, and I thought I would help clean the house. Why not feed my brother those unsightly cigarette butts from an ashtray that, for some unknowable reason, was on the floor? He ate the first with only a little protest. The next two took some work, and he was crying by the time I got them down. Mother came downstairs just as he started to vomit. I was interrogated and banished to the corner until we left for church.

One warm, sunny, summer afternoon we went to Gaston Park for a picnic. Mother got busy talking with other mothers and told me to keep an eye on my brother. The sand box seemed a safe place to play. My brother was just starting to walk, and the sand would be a nice cushion for his teetering gait. He loved it and was soon throwing handfuls into the air and laughing. I made a friend and told her my brother could eat sand. She was unimpressed until I gave him a spoonful. Wow, he did eat sand! That was all I needed. As my new friend watched raptly, I fed my brother spoonful after spoonful of that grainy dessert. I have no Idea how much he swallowed before Mother came to check on us. She was so mad, and my new friend was no help at all. She started saying how I forced him to eat the sand and made him cry.

My poor brother had sand in his diapers for 2 days. I know this because with every diaper change my mother would say, "This is all your fault."

Neshannock Walk

Jim Vallini

The Neshannock Creek eco-system on Pennsylvania's Allegheny Plateau drains the central portions of Mercer and Lawrence Counties and joins the Shenango River in New Castle. The pair continue south, are joined by the Mahoning River, which becomes the Big Beaver and all continue to the famous Ohio River. There are three designated Neshannock Creeks, the proper Neshannock; the Little Neshannock northwest; and Branch Little Neshannock farther west. They flow in the ledge rock conglomerate substructure of western Pennsylvania, bold and rapid, and drain about fifty square miles. Many channels, cricks, runs, and rills feed the streams. Most are not named, except as Nesha nock Creek, producing no end of Neshannocks in two counties.

Classified as an unaccessed stream, the Mercer-Lawrence waterway is mapped at Latitude 41 05' 21" and Longitude 80 18' 58" at its mouth in New Castle.

For perspective, begin my description of Neshannock Valley, with a summary of Lawrence County's river, the Shenango, Beaver tributary, about 100 miles long, west of the smaller Neshannocktreams. Shenango begins at the southern tip of Pymatuming Reservoir in Crawford County, flows to the village of Jamestown and continues south through Greene Township, fed by many runs. In Hempfield Township it flows through Greenville where it is joined by the Little Shenango River. The Little Shenango began in northeast Mercer County just off of Lake Wilhelm. It flowed west about 14 miles and met an assortment of cricks near Osgood, shifted south to meet big Shenango at Greenville. The joined streams continue south, leaving Hempfield and entering Pymatuming Townships. At Reynolds Heights it becomes the great oval string that comprises the Shenango river greenway and reservoirs. Continuing south Shenango makes its way along the western edge of Sharon, then leans southeast, enters Lawrence County, and forwards to New Castle. For its water volume it *is* unmatched in the region.

Neshannock Creek, subject of my treatise, begins withOtter Creek in upper Mercer County, which forms between Linn Tyro and Shay roads a mile or so below State Route 358. It flows a mile southwest to Bush Road, diverts southeast, and drifts to State Game Land #294 at Fredonia. Otter shifts south, meets two smaller components of Game Land #294, then approachesMercer.

Otter is joined east by Kents Run and then by northwestMunnell Run. Lastly, Cool Spring Creek, which origins northeast nearLake Latonka, fuses with Otter. Their union is muddled, the streams connecting and splitting, not fully merging until south of Mercer, East Lackawannock Township. A small lake on Mallard Way off of Lamor Road, west and above Mercer, begins asoutheast run that joins the mix. A half-mile further, west, Beaver Run joins the flux and Neshannock Creek continues its twenty-mile roll to New Castle.

But what is "neshannock"I puzzle. The name appears to exist already at the time of the Indian village of Kuskusky, a thriving Native American portal to the Beaver River and Ohio Valley, situated between the Creek and the Shenango River, where now is New Castle. Here the great rivers meld, Shenango, Mahoning, Beaver. The Kuskusky towns were many in the Allegheny plateau, and the one at New Castle was largest. They were peopled by the Seneca primarily, joined later by the Iroquois, then displaced from Virginia and retreating north. Trade lines were in place with the Delaware and Shawnee of eastern Pennsylvania, who were themselves being pushed west. Imposing on Indian Kuskuskys was colonial expansion, buffeted by British and French garrisons. The Indian struggle was for security and the preservation of cultural identity. The Kuskusky towns are noted in historical annals as early as 1748 for theircultural significance. But by the mid-1770s, ownership of theKuskusky lands passed from Indian to colonial.

Runs and creeks nurse the growing Neshannock. Pine Run from the east is next, then an unnamed run from the west.Interstate 80 crosses Neshannock, and below that sits the village of Hope Mills. At Hope, Old Mercer Road crosses the stream and meets Hope Mill and

Drake Roads. Pine Run joins from the east, just after the Creek departs Findley Township for Springfield Township. Downstream comes the village of Millburn andMillburn Road crosses. Further on, Mill Run, east, merges. After Mill Run, State Route 19 (Perry Highway) crosses the stream. Indian Run joins from the northwest, just above Leesburg Station, the last borough in Mercer County.

Neshannock starts as a Unami word. The Unami were Chippewa Indians who migrated east from Alberta, Montana, and Wyoming before the white invasion. They became the Lenni Lenape or Delaware Indians. "Neshannock" means two streams, or literally, the land between two waters. It is compound. *Nisha,* which means two, is attached to *Hene,* the root specifying "stream." Addedto the end is the locative suffix "k." And there *nishahenek* was born, its present spelling evolved through transliteration.

The geology of Neshannock valley is formed by glacial drift from Lake Erie to Wampum. The rocks include granite, gneiss, and feldspar mixed with limestone and sandstone. Structurally, the rocks demonstrate absences of folds and upward thrust. They belong to the Coal Measures, a division of the Upper Paleozoic Carboniferous period, when also formed the extensive workable coal beds. The coal beds are classified in the Mercergroup.

They were formed by the glacial period Wisconsin Ice Sheet. The summit between Nashannock valley and Shenango valley features Darlington Coal.

Ferriferous limestone is also highly valued in the region.

Limestone deposit formation and coal bed formation divides between the Upper and Lower Mercer groups. These signifiers correspond to lower Pennsylvanian bedrock stratigraphy.

Sandstone exists in two types. Much of the stream's course borders Tionesta Sandstone deposits. In New Castle thatbecomes Massillon Sandstone. Iron ore in the region is listed Lower Mercer Group.

The base soil is catalogued Pennsylvanian, formed 290-330 million years ago. It features cyclic sequences of sandstone, red and gray shale, conglomerate, coal, and limestone imbedded in a matrix of clay, fine sand, mud, and gravel. On hilltops the mass reaches to 40-50 feet thick. There are two classes of soil, that derived from the drift, and that from the decomposition of native coal measure rocks. Strong and rich are bothsoils. Ferriferous limestone, that with iron, is the element thatmakes the drift soil lush for crops, especially wheat, corn, oats.

Mining in the region concentrates in limestone, limonite, coal, and iron. Earth products include coal, clay, lime, and stone. The resident Ferriferous Limestone is considered most valuable. The favorability of locating natural gas resources in Devonian period and Paleozoic era shales is ranked moderately favorable to unfavorable. Geology sometimes imposes barriers to drilling. Lower Lawrence County features sizeable surface and near-surface distribution of Vanport limestone, which offers high calcium.

The presence of immense ledge rock structure in Lawrence County leads to terraced landscape. Nashannock stream is alternately terraced with summits rising, or not terraced, forming field or farm. The New Castle plat features three terraces, moving west. The low Terrace upon which the city sits is first. Across the Shenango, the second terrace rises. The third, higher, continues west.

We're not to those terraces yet, my friend. Here only the beginning of Lawrence County. It was formed in 1848 from parts of Mercer and Beaver Counties. Lawrence was named for Admiral James Lawrence whose contribution to history occurred during the 1813 Battle of Boston Bay when he cried out, Don't give up the ship!" In Lawrence County, the stream rolls through Wilmington Township first, which measures 19.91 square miles and counts a 2016 population of 2,632. The two cities on the Lawrence County north border include New Wilmington and Volant. Both feature a Neshannock Creek link. The Little Neshannock, also originating in Mercer County, follows the eastern rim of New Wilmington rolling due south. The proper Neshannock follows the west rim of Volant and moves southwest. The two streams merge at Mayville, still in Wilmington Township.

Volant at 1,033 feet above sea level lists a population of 168,000. Route 208, or Main Street, features quaint specialty shops and Neshannock Creek Inn, which offers traditional American cuisine. There are two wineries in the city, both on Main Street, the Volant

Winery and the Knockin Noggin Cidery & Winery. The historic Volant Mill established in 1812 and the mid-century railroad boom generated a flourishing business district late nineteenth and early twentieth centuries. The Amish community is nearby. Neshannock Creek below Volant sports excellent trout and fly fishing. Also, Neshannock Creek Trail offers 4.1 miles of moderately trafficked out and back trail with scenic views; use for hiking, walking, nature trips, birding; best used March to October. Route 208 crosses the Creek. Potter Run merges from the east. Another mile the creek forms a small lake serviced by Lake Road. Now the stream reaches Neshannock Falls and Banks Covered Bridge. From the north, Covered Bridge Road meets Neshannock at the bridge and becomes Eastbrook Neshannock Falls Road across the stream. Banks Covered Bridge was opened in 1889. It spans the creek southeast and features the Burr Arch Truss System with reinforced steel undergirding. Measures 121 feet in length and is painted white.

Now the stream approaches Neshannock Waterfall, a wild and romantic spot, visited by pleasure parties. The fall is formed by a No. XII slate ledge. Below the falls, Route 956 crosses the Neshannock on its way to New Wilmington. It follows the Creek for a half-mile until Neshannock turns abruptly south and State 956 continues northwest and crosses the Little Neshannock.

Next is the borough of Mayville, west and north of the Creek. Here there is some looping of the stream and a shift west about four miles. Between the boroughs, Sipe Road falls from the north due south, crosses the stream and meets Lakewood Nashannock Falls Road. The Creek at Mayville, still in Wilmington Township, absorbs Little Neshannock Creek rolling south from New Wilmington. Before they merge, the Little exhibits a water web as complex as the mother steam, theLittle already having combined with Branch Neshannock, thethird sibling, back in Mercer County.

What residents call Little Neshannock Creek actually begins two miles north of the latitude where Otter Creek and Beaver Run meet to start Nashannock Creek proper. The Little begins west of Highland Road in Jefferson Township, just above Lamar Road, with a modest curl as proper with stream beginnings. It crosses Lamar and drops south until it meets Branch a half mile before Lawrence County begins. Flowing south it is crossed by Sharon- Mercer Road (US 62) and stops Old Sharon Road. It parallels Flat Road and moves into Lackawanna Township. Next, Route 318.

(Mercer-West Middlesex Road) crosses. The stream continues until Interstate 80 crosses. Here, Pulaski-Mercer Road crosses, and a mile farther, Harthegig Run joins the Little from the west. Now south flow is uninterrupted until the Little meets Branch Neshannock Creek.

Branch begins in Lackawanna Township a couple miles west of Little Neshannock and a mile below Margaree Run, which falls north into the great Shenango Reservoir. From a humble two- pronged beginning off Frogtown Road in Lackawannock Township, Branch moves west two miles and right turns abruptly south. Now in Sharon City, it clips only the southeast corner. In the townships, Branch zigzags south and southeast, clipping Lackawanna, Shenango, then Lackawanna again, before landing in Wilmington Township and its meeting with the Little, about seven miles extension.

The same major highways that intersect the Little cross Branch; Mercer West Middlesex Road, Interstate 80, and Pulaski Mercer Road. Wilmington Road very closely follows Branch west side, although the roadway name changes, starting out as South Neshannock Road at Frogtown, where it picks up the Branch; it becomes Bethel Wilmington Road and then Bethel New Wilmington Road. Villages include Bethel and Carbon in Lackawannock Township, and Lyle in Wilmington. County roads crossing the Branch include Greenfield Road at Carbon and Bend Road at Lyle.

Geography is enriched, note, by the grace of flora and fauna thriving in Neshannock watershed. Pennsylvania state divides into three flora provinces. Neshannock system is in the Allegheny plateau. Plant life is primarily herbaceous leaf plants, both angiosperm and gymnosperm, which references mostly if the seed is in an ovary or naked. Protecting plant life are deciduous trees, shrubs, bushes, and woody vines. The stream hosts leafy aquatic plants, both surface and submerged. Included are marine vegetables, seaweeds, water grasses, water lilies, ferns, moss. Mosses include Clubmoss and Spikemoss; ferns feature Horse-tail and Adder's Tongue, Royal and Serpentine. Wetlands capture Cattails, Sedge, Violets, Mint. The pasture homes diverse grasses, plants, herbs, wildflowers, fruits. Small trees, nut trees, large trees, shrubs puff thewoods.

Stream and field wetlands exhibit Arrowhead, or Duck Potatoes; Duckweed, Horsetail, Jewelweed, Reed Grass, Cinquefoil, Labrador Tea, Pickerel Weed, Spatterdock, and the Yellow Pond Lily. In the field and pasture look for edibles like Ramps, or Wild Leeks; also Wild Rice, Watercress, Sunflowers, wild garlic, Wild Onions and Chives, Wild Anise. Bush and ground fruits include Strawberry, Blackberry, Blueberry, Boysenberry, Raspberry, Elderberry, Gooseberry, Cranberry, Grape, and Current. Wild natural field and pasture tenants include Clover, Stinging Nettle, Daylillies, Sorrel, Purslane, Dandelion, Chickweed, Beebalm, and many Mushroom species. Along roadways notice Chicory, Clover, Primrose. In fields, Goatsbeard, Heal All, Sun Choke, Pigweed, Milkweed, Plantain, Spiderwort, Thistle, Black Mustard, Autumn Olive, Carrion Flower; Chinese Lantern, or Ground Cherry; Mayapple, Wild Rose, Spicebush, Wintergreen, Water Lily. These are friendly and benign species, but many of our pasture relatives are poisonous. Handle carefully Liverwort, Arrow Arum, Baneberry, Bugbane, Nightshade, Sumac, Skunk Cabbage, Buckthorn, Jimsonweed, Dutchman's Breeches, Foxglove, Hemlock, Hellebore, Horse Nettle, Jack-In- The-Pulpit. or Indian Turnip; Larkspur; Lobelia, or Indian Tobacco; Mayapple; Milkweed, Moonseed, Poison Ivy, poison oak, pokeweed, skunk cabbage, sumac, and water Hemlock.

Do not be dismayed, friend. So many species, so many roles to play, and some of these denizens remote or unusual, so that much looking is required to find. Look for Bedstraw, more properly known as Cleavers. This wild plant is edible, the leaves for salad, tea as a diuretic, even for eczema. The seeds can be ground as a coffee substitute, better than chicory. A common fern is the Maidenhair, also called Fiddleheads. Wild ginger is prolific, the root is aromatic. Other edible wild plants include the Groundnut, Indian Cucumber; Marsh Marigold, or Cowslip; the Rue or Wood Anemone, of the Buttercup family; Solomon's seal; Spring Beauty, also known as the Indian or Mountain Potato; the brown-skinned corm is edible; skin and wash, eat raw or cooked; Wild Anise, or Sweet Cicely; Toothwort, Trillium, Trout Lily. These are edible, or have medicinal application. Other plants are potentially problematic. For instance, common to the valley is Pokeweed, and the poisonous pokeberry. Find the plant on the fringe of woods; its long curving fruit stem shows large black poisonous berries on a purple stem. The recipes for pokeweed salad limit to the leaves, which for best safety, pick before the stems turn purple.

The tree canopy, is dominated by twelve species, including Beech, Elm, Sycamore, Black Cherry, Eastern Red Oak, Hemlock, Hickory, Red Maple, Sugar Maple, Sassafras, White Oak, Yellow Birch. Look also for the Ohio Buckeye, or Horse Chestnut; Allegheny Serviceberry, or Juneberry; Black Birch, Sweet Birch, Alder, Black Elder, Hawthorn, Juniper, Persimmon, Butternut, Chestnut, Walnut, Black Walnut, and American Hornbeam. Small trees include Mountain Ash, Paw Paw, Red Chokeberry, Buttonbush, Redbud; Pagoda, Silky, Gray, and Flowering Dogwoods; Hazelnut, Witch-Hazel, and Wild Hydrangea. Typical are fruit trees, Apple, Pear, Cherry. Many are the varieties of Evergreen, starting with Spruce, Eastern White Pine, Pinyon Pine, Pitch Pine, Red Pine, and Virginia Pine. Smaller shrubs include Sumac, also poisonous; Abelia, Azalea, Saint John's Wort, and New Jersey Tea.

Our fauna landscape shows Seventy-one mammal species living in Pennsylvania, eleven of those no longer found. Dominant still are Bear, Deer, Elk, Wolves. The Gray Fox roams widely. Also find the Red Fox, which is not native. All manner of ground furbearers roam, including Muskrat, Mink, Beaver, Possum, Striped Skunk, Otter, Raccoon, Rabbit, Mole, and Shrew. Most numerate multiple sub-species. Two species of mole take residence, the Hoary-towed and Star-nosed. The mouse-like Shrew is diverse, including Water, Smoky, Masked, Rock, Pygmy, Short-tailed, and Least Shrews. Rabbits, on the other hand, feature the Eastern Cottontail in Neshannock valley, which populates most of the United States. Our popular flying mammal, the bat, shows numerous variety, the little Brown Bat, Big Brown Bat, Evening, Silver-haired, Red, Honey, Pygmy; Keen, which is also called the Pink Bat; Leib, which is rare; and the Indiana Bat, which is endangered.

Bird species in western Pennsylvania number 414. Regular denizens count to 285, with 129 less frequent visitors. Along the stream encounter Ducks, Geese, Swans and other waterfowl. The insect population in Pennsylvania numbers 587 common insects. 645 varieties have been observed. Aquatic insects include those that live in the water and those disposed to leaving their larvae in the water. Along the Creek find the

Water Bug, a true specie, not a generic term. Also, the Dragonfly, Mayfly, Stonefly, Dobsonfly, Caddisfly, Damselfly, and many more.

Now close to the water, I am reminded that my gentle stream is more than hydrogen and oxygen. Looks so clear and pristine through simple eyes, formless, and yet I remember the complexity of the phylum Protozoa, that microscopic universe in just a drop of water, single-cell organisms reproducing and generating bacteria, good or coliform. Waterfowl are dependent on the permanent body of water and open feeding areas. Swans eat aquatic plants; geese eat terrestrial grasses. The Mallard is a common resident, as it is broadly in North America; they are filter feeders and will consume almost anything edible.

In the bacterial brew of our stream live numerous fish species. Stocked stream portions include Cool Spring Creek near Mercer and Lawrence County beneath Volant. Bass and Trout are popular, including Small and Largemouth; Brown and Rainbow. Find also Yellow Perch; various Sunfish, especially Bluegill; Channel Catfish, Walleye, Northern Pike, Stream Pike, Steelhead, Muskellunge, Pickerel, Brown Bullhead, Black Crappie; Golden Shiners, a large minnow species; Flathead Minnows; and Darters, which are small bottom-dwelling foragers. For anglers, the stocked sections are classified "Delayed Harvest," which allows closed and open fishing seasons. In Pennsylvania fishing is permitted, with license, June 1 to September 30. Fishing October to May is catch and release. Licenses are available on-line only. For information, www.fishandbait.com

The first major fishing venue in the Neshannock system is along Cool Spring Creek near Mercer. This is classified a Delayed Harvest Artificial Lures Only area, stocked with brown and rainbow trout. A listing describes as spectacular the delayed harvest stretch from a wire across the stream at abandoned road to Scrubgrass Road. Also in Mercer County, tryCreek Road where Route 19 crosses the stream. Branch Little Neshannock, north of Bend Road, is also stocked with trout.

The area stretching from the base of Mill Dam in Volant downstream to the covered bridge at Covered Bridge Road (Township Road 476) is stocked with Brown and Rainbow Trout. Annual stocking day is in March. It is another Delayed Harvest Artificial Lures Only area and under private ownership. Below Neshannock Falls a mile whitewater run offers one of the best trout fishing venues in western Pennsylvania. This is class I to II whitewater with calm fishing and swimming holes between.

The hub for angler service is the Neshannock Creek FlyShop on Main Street in Volant. On its website, May 5, 2018 at 4:00 PM it posted, stream conditions are great and the stream fished well today." The store offers upper end high-quality fishing gear and tying materials for fly fishing. Accommodations offered at the FlyShop include a boat launch, and fishing schools for young anglers, female anglers, and fly-fishing.

Fishing is recreational. Include also in our pursuit of Neshannock recreation boating, kayaking, swimming, hiking, running, camping, sight-seeing, and picnicing. After Volant, the Neshannock Gorge whitewater rapids begin a kayak and tube run of about two miles. It is ranked a class II run; for craft floating the rapids, the difficulty range is I-II. It flushes about eightrapids in a mile stretch. The flow range is 1800 to 4000 CFS (cubic feet per second). The put-in is at the covered bridge on Covered Bridge Road, north of Route 956. If the water level is up, you can put-in back at Volant and float two extra miles before you reach the covered bridge. The take-out is at the new bridge where 956 draws close to the stream, or you can continue another four miles to the parking lot at Neshannock Falls.

Let me take you on a kayak float. Meet me at Abby Lane where State Route 956 crosses the stream. The creek starts slow, has some riffles, Class I flow. We pass under the 956 bridge, scoot through a wooded area, turn right, and pass two old stone bridge abutments; rapids start at this turn, the bigger rapids only fifty yards downstream from the falls; they are shaped by eroded ledges; there are large boulders to dodge; feel large wave train sections where the creek drops steadily; the run feels isolated; it's a narrow wooded valley with no buildings or roads visible; Amish vicinity; a popular stocked trout stream, there are fisherman near the bridges; all private land, no camping; a fallen tree is a hazard, creates blockage.

Overall, Neshannock Creek has four prominent water trails. First is below Volant to the Falls. Next is where the Creek is joined by Little Neshannock, and water volume almost doubles.

Another trail creates when eastern Hettenbaugh Lake and long Hettenbaugh Run meets Neshannock at Painter Hill to create the very short Hottenbaugh Run, which pushes the stream directly west for a mile, and then abruptly shifts south at right angle in an area absent natural landmarks. The final water trail begins where Mckee Crossing ends at the Creek and the Neshannock shifts southeast from its direct north fall to begin its descent into New Castle City. Water flow is restrained in New Castle, but river enthusiasts can walk, hike, or run another Neshannock land Trail, with trailhead north of Route 65 and continuing to Oak Park Cemetery.

Other Neshannock recreation venues feature amenities. For bread & breakfast, try Pine Hills Inn on Old Mercer Road; or overnight at Candleford Inn on Mercer Street, both in Volant. Green Meadows Golf Course is also in Volant. Equestrian enthusiasts meet at the Little Neshannock stables in New Wilmington near Little Neshannock. Lakewood Park amusements is located in Painter Hill. A Bicycle PA-Route V Trail parallels the stream south to the Little and crosses Neshannock in New Castle close to the Shenango junction.

I have paused in my walk to review distinguished landmarks and must regain my footing. Branch, now at Bend Road in Lyle, loops east a mile to meet the north-south Little Neshannock.

North of the junction, State Route 158 (Mercer-New Wilmington Road) crossed over both Branch and Little Neshannock creeks. The Little, with Branch, continues south, flows by the eastern edge of New Wilmington, and is fed by six alternating runs, east, west, east, and on, all named Little Neshannock Creek, the last run at the bottom of the Wilmington City boundary.

It would be proper for my reader to assume Neshannock valley owns agricultural heritage. The soil is productive, prized crops include grains and vegetables. Notice the milemarker on Shaw Road at SR 1004 in New Wilmington, just below the Mercer line. It acknowledges former resident Neshannock Potato, cultivated on the farm of John and James Gilkey, Irish immigrants, first producing the potato in 1797. It was grown and marketed widely in the nineteenth century, a choice variety.

Also called the Mercer and the Gilkey potato, the Neshannock was reddish-purple, with same-colored streaks through the flesh, which disappeared when the vegetable was cooked.

Wilmington Township is also Lawrence County's Amish region.

In 1849, Old Order Amish from Mifflin County, middle Pennsylvania, migrated west to New Castle. Finding the area hospitable, Amish families trekked north and settled in Wilmington Township, now home to probably Pennsylvania's largest Old Order Amish community. The village of New Wilmington had been platted in 1824, before the migration, but was not formally established as borough until April 9, 1863. The 2010 census populated it at 2,466. It occupies 1.1 miles of land.

What we specify Amish territory begins east with County Route 168 and Volant. North it broadens beyond Route 208 into Mercer County and reaches to where Little Neshannock and Branch Neshannock meet. South, they populate below County Route 956 to the border of Wilmington Township and beyond. They occupy west beyond Pulaski and County Road 551. They came to Wilmington about 2,000 strong. Now they comprise fourteen church districts. The average family has seven children; youth begin daily chores at age seven.

The Amish are a traditionally dressed hard-working rural population, and Christian separatists. The men grow a beard when they marry, and always wear a hat. Women dress primarily in blue; they close their garment with snaps or hooks, even straight pins, buttons being too showy. Women, too, always wear a head covering. Their language is Pennsylvania Dutch, a dialect of German, spoken at home. Children are taught English when they begin school.

Culturally, they offer baked goods, cooking, quilts, rugs, handcrafts, toys, candles, soaps, furniture, home and barn building, and respect for the environment. In their Pennsylvania community you will find hand-painted signs, a private schoolhouse, a cemetery, shops, auctions, homes, and barns. They build their own homes and do not use electricity. Additions to houses are small detached dwellings called "dowdy" houses, where grandparents live. The children are Amish home-schooled at one of seventeen parochial schools in the area, 25 to 30 children each, grades one to eight. They must pass a difficult eighth grade proficiency test.

The Amish auction house is located on Route 208 in New Wilmington. Amish and English farmers meet, socialize, purchase or trade goods, livestock, and kerosene. Transportation is provided by the common horse & buggy. Brown-capped buggies are unique to Lawrence

County. For distance travel the Amish will ride a bus or hire a vehicle. The Amish graveyard is small and nondescript, behind a white gate at the intersection of Auction Road and High Street outside New Wilmington. The smaller area Mennonite community also uses the cemetery. The Amish are remembered by small stones.

The Amish community is watered by Little Neshannock Creek rolling south along the east rim of New Wilmington and continuing south. The Creek passes the village of Fayette and borders Cottage Grove. At Cottage Grove another west run joins and Old Mercer Road crosses the Little. Just on, Route 956 crosses. Now we are in Mayville and proper Neshannock Creek, moving west, merges with the Little.

Proper Neshannock's meander through Lawrence County after Volant visited a lake, covered bridge, and falls in Neshannock Falls Township, Village, and Camp. This is a leisure stretch of the Creek. The Camp listed for short-term rental in April of 2019 a three-bedroom, two-bath cottage with 1500 feet of creek frontage. The "falls" is a popular attraction at a tip in the southwest rolling stream where the waterway shifts northwest for less than a mile until the village of Mayville. County road Sipe parts the villages north of the stream. Sipe crosses the creek and becomes Lakewood Neshannock Falls Road. The Neshannock at Mayville, still in Wilmington Township, merges with the Little and the pair continue south, now between Neshannock Township, west, and Hickory Township, east. At the juncture, the Little continues south, while the proper Neshannock shifts south from its southwest fall.

In 2016, Neshannock Township listed a population of 9,293. It encompasses an area of 17.42 square miles and borders west a quarter mile before the Shenango River, where begins Pulaski Township. East of the stream, Hickory Township plats an area of 15.93 square miles, and lists a population in 2016 of 2,632 with a total of 925 households. Continuing another mile-and-a-half sits the village of Sunset Valley. At Grahms village, next, another west run feeds the stream, and the Neshannock borders, about a quarter mile, State Game Land #178. Just on, another small lake positions, and now visit the village of Painter Hill.

At Painter Hill Neshannock meets Hottenbaugh and Hettenbaugh Runs, west/east. At the join, Hettenbaugh Run becomes Hottenbaugh. East Maitland Lane crosses the streams. The Runs and Creek turn south and continue the southerly Nashannock migration. Notice a small lake on Hettenberg Run just east of the merge. Also find Lakewood Park. The proper stream flows southwest, now rural and natural. Peluso Camp sits at McKee Crossing Road. The stream becomes part of the border of Graceland Cemetery, curls away from the cemetery, circles back, and becomes the border of Oak Park Cemetery, now as a long thin lake. Here Neshannock Creek is in the city limits of New Castle.

City streets now intersect with the stream. First crosses Dillworth Avenue which joins Neshannock Avenue Extension. An unnamed crick joins the stream from the east. Neshannock Avenue follows the stream south, west bank. Other side, Croton Avenue (State Route 108) follows the stream north to Cleveland Avenue, then veers east. Walk south again and Croton Avenue follows the stream past Jefferson Street. Shortly before the Creek meets the Shenango, Croton crosses the stream and becomes the Columbus Interbelt, which ends abruptly at West Falls Street after paralleling the Shenango River for several city blocks. Before this point Neshannock Creek was crossed by East North Street, which ends at Croton; East Washington (State Route 65); Mill Street, North becoming South; Lawrence Street, which becomes Grove; and finally South Jefferson.

I am walking down Jefferson, sign says South, towards East/West Washington Street. Where did civil engineer John Carlyle Stewart stand when he claimed fifty New Castle acres inside the Neshannock-Shenango V, I wonder? Lawrence County lands had been designated "homestead right" for veterans of the Revolutionary War that wished to pioneer. The "lands" had been surveyed. For whatever motivation or commission, John Stewart resurveyed those "lands" and determined that a fifty-acre parcel between the Shenango and Neshannock had been omitted from the original survey. Being outside of existing claims, and being a sensible man, Stewart claimed the acres for himself. John Stewart then laid out the town of New Castle in April 1798.

My thoughts running. In 1840 the population of New Castle was only 611. By the 1870s, the growing gateway town counted over 6,000 inhabitants. I wonder where New Castle's canals connected during the same period canal era, 1833 to 1871. New Castle had three canal hubs. Mine product, limestone, building rock, coal were eager transport customers. Wagons were slow and costly. The canals included the Beaver

Division, the one canal that crossed the Neshannock. It extended thirty miles, from Charles Mill at Beaver on the Ohio River to six miles north of New Castle on the Shenango River. Next, the Erie Division started at the Shenango hub of the Beaver Division and extended to Erie Pennsylvania, 106 miles. Also, the Pennsylvania and Ohio Canal started two miles south of New Castle and followed the Mahoning River to Akron Ohio, where it joined the Erie Canal.

The Mahoning channel was also known as the Cross Cut Canal. The canals were also linked to Pittsburgh, and from there to Pennsylvania's Main Line Canal, which began east as Union Canal at the Delaware River.

Still walking, I approach a monument, the intersection of Jefferson and East Washington. Civil War. All the great battles are listed, 1861-1865. Lawrence County war dead are listed by name. Lincoln's Gettysburg Address is included. The monument is signed by Soldiers & Citizens of Lawrence County in tribute to The War Of The Rebellion. A separate smaller installation commemorates Lawrence County World War l dead, 1914-1918.

Just past the monument, I turn east, my left, pace two blocks. The blocks are short, the width of buildings. I'm on East, follow it to Mill Street, which I'm attracted to for the nostalgia of its name. East curves away and ridges the Neshannock, a building and patio sitting up above the creek. From Mill I can see building tenants, 2 Rivers and the Dirty Pickle. This is a fashionable modern building, which seems, I discover, to have some history, the structure called Riverplex. I determine to visit the Dirty Pickle, on the creek side of the building, ground floor. The lobby stretches up to roof. Second story is recessed, with circular balcony locating businesses. Artsy. There is a nightclub on the balcony and a stylist.

At the Pickle, I order their $3 Best Coffee In The World. It isn't. Theirs is the patio on the bank. I go outside. There are black steel tables and chairs. We had a set like these at home growing up. Seated, I see the creek clearly, its depth low, its bottom, stones. I reckon Shenango, to my right, is about six or eight city blocks away. I look again at the bottom stones.

They are sizeable, volleyballs and larger. The water is clean, clear. I think of the Indian word, Seneca, our early population. It translates literally to "it has stones." How perfect.

I adjust my reflection as I sip my coffee to local history. New Castle heroes include the Warner Brothers. At this riverplex was located their first theater. Harry, Sam, and Albert Warner began constructing that theater in a much different building in1906. It sat ninety-nine, three movies for a nickel. Sixteen years later Warner Brothers Pictures was established.

The breeze picks up, it's blowing the pages of my notepad.I secure them and walk to the patio's edge, lean against the retaining wall. I am about fifteen feet above the water. The crick is some sixty feet wide, I am sure. There's a little capping, the flow brisk.

Directly across the river, just right, is an old three- story warehouse, maybe seventy-five feet wide. It might be shut- up. Ground level there are several closed garage doors. Higher up a painted-on brick sign, white letters on black, reads R.E. Whittacker Co. Underneath it says Roto Wash. What's a roto-wash, I puzzle. Two geese sail by, moving up creek. One gobbles. Roto is short for rotor, I remember. Which attaches to rotate. so I muse thoughts of washing machines or spraying systems. Thank you, Mr. Whittaker, for letting me presume.

My coffee finished, I figure to return to Mill Street and cross the crick. Middle of the bridge and mid-Neshannock, I observe other side the Jefferson Poultry shop, also on Mill Street. It seems open for business. A garage door is up. Yellow "Jefferson Poultry" trucks mill about. Across the street, I see a Salvation Army thrift store. I wonder about New castle discards. I look back downstream and wonder if I can see the Shenango from here. I don't think. It's very peaceful. There's little population about. Few cars.

I smile, look at my map, look downstream again. After Neshannuck meets Shenango, one more run joins the parade to the Mahoning River. Big Run, east, about ten miles long, begins about the longitude of the New Castle cemeteries, and is a considerable little stream. It flows southweet, cuts through Cascade and Cunningham Parks, just south of New Castle, loops around and proceeds north to meet the Shenango.

Now the Neshannock tributary web is complete and Shenango-Neshannock flows briskly to the Mahoning.

You are entitled, dear reader, to some restatement of the facts and reflections here offered. Pointed out are the various runs and cricks that feed the Neshannock, a native word meaning "between two streams." Functionally, those two streams must be the Shenango and Mahoning Rivers, although in any cartographic sense, the Neshannock system is not between the two rivers, Various boroughs populate the illustrated cricks, proper Neshannock Creek, Little Neshannock Creek, and Branch Neshannock Creek. These traverse together plus fifty miles offering scenic wonder, recreation, towns and boroughs, connecting roadways, a mesh of tributaries, landscape and wildlife, and history.

Integrated waterways, I emphasize in closure, create an eco-system, connect fragmented habitats, and so conserve biodiversity. This I have attempted to demonstrate with my review of the geography, surface hydrology, and cultural legacy of the Neshannock Creeks, between two streams. Let me finish with a simple call, my friends, please use, honor, respect, and conserve the Neshannock Creeks.

Bibliography

G.M. Johnson and Associates Ltd. (AAA). City Street Map, Lawrence County, Mercer County. Vancouver, BC. 2016.

Higbee, Howard William. *Stream Map of Pennsylvania.* Pennsylvania State University. State College, Pa. 1965.

https://www.americanwhitewater.org/content/River/detail/id/3121/ *American Whitewater.* 2019.

https://www.google.com.

Meuninck, Jim. Edible *Wild Plants and Useful Herbs. Falcon Guides.* Morris Book Publishing, Guilford, Connecticut. 2013.

Rhoads, Ann Fowler and Timothy A. Block. *The Plants of Pennsylvania, 2nd ed.* University of Pennsylvania Press, Philadelphia. 2000.

Scialabba, Adolph. *History of Canals In Lawrence County.*

Graduate Faculty, Slippery Rock State College. June 1965.

Shultz, Charles H. Ed. *The Geology of Pennsylvania.* Pennsylvania Geological Survey/Pittsburgh Geological Society. 1999.

Visit Lawrence County. Visit Lawrence County Pennsylvania,

Visitors Guide. New Castle, Pa. 2018. https://www.visitlawrencecounty.com

White, I.C. *The Geology of Lawrence County; A Special Report on The Coal Measures in Western Pennsylvania and Eastern Ohio* [Dissertation; Rare Books]. Commissioners, Second Geological Survey, Harrisburg. 1877.

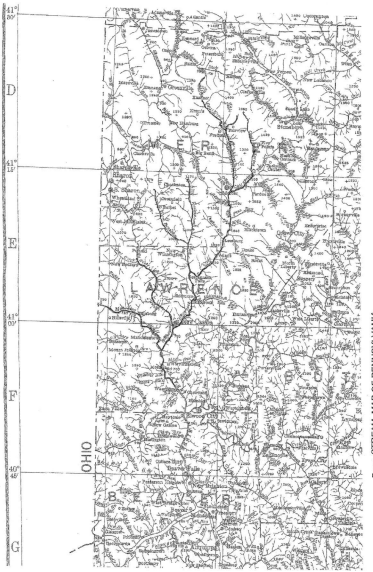

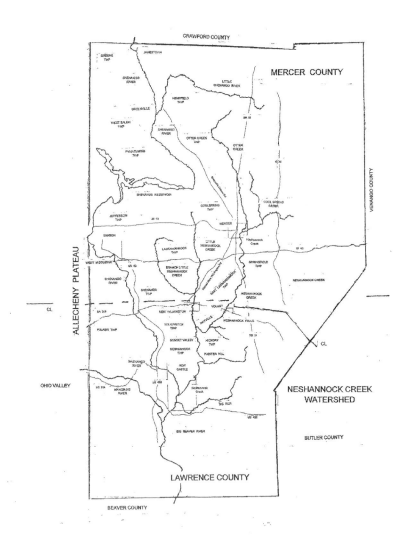

On Sunny Lane

Dorothy Knight Burchett

I didn't always live on Sunny Lane. In fact, I didn't always live anywhere, but the last place I lived was on Huckleberry Ridge. I wrote a newspaper column there for 12 years, until the format of the newspaper changed and I moved on to other things.

I still lived on Huckleberry Ridge, though, until my first husband passed away and I met someone else who became my husband. His name is Bob, but I call him Sweetheart. He thinks that is a term of endearment, but it's more than that. It's my safety net, so I don't call him by the wrong name. That's how I came to move to Sunny Lane, because that's where his houseis. Actually it wasn't here until he built it and we moved in shortly thereafter.

Our lane shouldn't be called Sunny Lane, though. It got its name from the next door neighbor, back in the day when the township officials were going from doo to door and asking the oldest resident on the lane or road what they would like to call it. Sweetheart's neighbor, at the time, decided to call it after her cat—her dead cat. It could be worse, though. It could be named after one of our cats. How does Flopsie Lane, or Skittles Lane sound? I don't think so.

No. I think it should be called Walnut Tree Lane. There must be 20 of them, from the bottom of the lane to the top of the hill, in various stages of development. Some of them are productive, though. In the fall, I gather the walnuts off the ground, put on my plastic gloves and husk them. I wash them off and put them in a cage to dry, so the squirrels won't help themselves to them. My husband uses vise grips and cracks them in the winter. Now, most people who have walnut trees in their yards think they are a nuisance. they run over themwith the lawn mower and they have to pick them up and discard them. Not us. It may be a lot of work, but there's nothing better than to bite into a piece of carrot cake or chocolate chip cookie containing black walnuts.

When I lived on Huckleberry Ridge, I thought it was the best place to live. I had lived there for 42 years. I knew all of the people who lived along that road. I planted a garden and fruit trees. I oversaw and helped with remodeling the house through the years and saw a great transformation take place. I raised three children there. I told my first husband I wasn't moving from there until I was in my own box (my casket). As I was pulling out of the driveway for my last trip to my new home, I put a cardboard box on the front seat, got in and my new husband drove away.

Well, now I think Sunny Lane is the best place to live. When I taught Summer Bible School, years ago, we played a little song for the children called, "Bloom Where You're Planted". It told them how we sometimes wish we could live somewhere else, or have different circumstance, but to make the most of where you are and to be the best person you can be, no matter where you are.

It might be good advice no matter how old a person is.

Previously published in *New Castle News* and *Progress Weekly*, Emlenton, PA.

Nineteen Nineteen

Susan Urbanek Linville

Sophie Johnson and I waited for our husbands, John and Frank. Across the street, the American Sheet and Tin Plate Company rumbled and belched black soot into the gray afternoon sky. Men exited the Hobart Street gate, just getting off from their 12-hour shift. They trudged toward the southside neighborhood, a sea of sweat and grime, happy to be on their way home, or maybe somewhere else to grab a beer. Hunkys, Dagos, Polaks, Krauts. They were all there. Even a few Jews like us, and Fins, like the Johnsons.

A trolley coasted by, electric lines snapping and popping like a toaster. It reminded me that I'd promised Mrs. Williams, the old widow living next door, that I'd pick up some bread for her at the market.

Sophie's husband, John, being taller than most, was easy to spot in the crowd. Frank followed with Benny Lavorozi and Levi De Prano. Other men looked familiar, but I didn't know their names. It was probably better not to know everyone. Supporting the union wasn't the safest choice in New Castle. Work your hours, go home to your families, and take what we give you was the rule of thumb. Be happy you have work. If you didn't like it, you could go back to your own country.

Sophie wore her long blond hair tied up and disguised beneath a floppy hat. I wore a plaid scarf and my old grey dress. Despite that, John walked directly to us. "There's a change of plans," he said. His blue eyes scanned the houses lining the street.

"What's wrong?" Sophie asked.

Frank tipped his cap back. "Word's out. The mill's got spies."

"You think they know about Nick's?" Sophie asked. We'd been meeting at Nick Asianides' billiard hall on Moravia Street for months. By now, everyone at the mill knew about us.

"They're worried we're going to strike with the rest of 'em tomorrow," John said. "Let's head home and meet at Gus' in two hours."

"Mary and I will let the women know," Sophie said.

Gus' billiard hall wasn't as popular as others along Long Avenue. Gus ran a tight ship and wouldn't tolerate too much drinking or even a hint that a fight might break out. After working in the heat all day, if the mill guys wanted to blow off steam, Gus' wasn't the place.

A cool September breeze was blowing through town by the time we reached Long Avenue. The sun had already set, but the sky glowed orange above the mill fires.

Gus wasn't too happy to see a group of ten women in heeled shoes clomping into his establishment. We were trouble with a capital T, but we didn't care. If the last two years had taught us anything, it was that women had every right to stand up and have their say. Jeannette Rankin of Montana had been the first woman elected to the House of Representatives two years before. When Woodrow Wilson ran for president, the Democratic Party platform supported women's suffrage.

Even though Alice Paul, leader of the National Woman's Party, had been put in solitary confinement in a prison mental ward to "break" her will and undermine her credibility, we all knew she was just as sane as the rest of us. Just recently, the National Woman's Party picketed in front of the White House holding banners. We were following in the footsteps of picketers who were sentenced to up to six months in jail and would take our chances.

Sophie led the way between tables to the back of the bar where there was a private room. A couple of drunk, grease covered men cat called.

"Why don't you gals git back to yer sewin'? a man growled.

I stopped.

Did they think their wives and children were not suffering because of their long hours and low wages? Did they think we had nothing to offer? Bastards.

Sophie grabbed my hand. "Come on," she said. "Ignore them."

It didn't take long for the gathering to be standing-room-only. Men gave up their seats at the card tables to the ladies. Sophie worked her way to the back and stood with a handful of papers gathered to her breast.

Strike. No one was saying the word, but the air was thick with it.

"Can I have your attention," Sophie said.

The room quieted.

"Today, The National Committee for Organizing Iron and Steel Workers called for a strike."

Not everyone in the room understood English. A couple of the women translated as Sophie spoke about Mother Jones, a schoolteacher who founded the IWW and organized the mine workers. "Only by being organized can we bring change," Sophie said. "Striking one mill at a time achieves nothing. This is to be a national strike. The owners will listen to us if all the mills are shut down."

"What about riots?" an balding gentleman asked. "Men 'ill be killed."

It was a good question. More than 100 people were injured during the Youngstown riot, triggered by a strike three years before. Stores were looted, fires destroyed buildings and houses. People had also been shot and killed in Pittsburgh. Most of us had children, including Sophie who had two young daughters. We wanted a peaceful strike.

"Tell me, Dominic," Sophie said. "How well can you feed and clothe your family making 75 cents an hour? Coffee is up to 47 cents a pound. Bacon is 45 cents. Do you only eat beef that chews like shoe leather? Can you afford $1.00 pants for your sons?"

"We work to make the fat cats fatter," a man behind me called out. "It's time we got fair pay."

The crowd applauded.

"Low pay is better than no pay," another man said. "I can't afford to get fired."

"That's why we need to work together." Sophie slid a photograph from her stack of papers. "August 26th, Fanny Sellins gave up her life in West Natrona. She didn't have to join the picket line, but she wanted to fight for you, and me, for all of us. She wanted to help you receive higher wages and better working conditions."

Sophie passed a photograph to the nearest man. "When Mrs. Sellins tried to help a wounded striker, she was shot in the back by a deputy, and if that wasn't enough, he used a cudgel to bash in her skull."

The photograph showed Fanny's body lying on a coroner's table covered to the neck in a white sheet. Her skull was flattened from the crown of her head to her eyebrows. Some stared, others barely glanced at the shocking image.

"It is our time," Sophie said. "We must stand up for our rights."

"Strike!" A man called out.

"Strike!" the crowd joined in. "Strike! Strike! Strike!" They poured out of the bar and into the street ready to form a picket line.

It was almost three-o-clock in the afternoon, Monday, September 22nd. I waited for Sophie on her front porch with a basket of sandwiches and apples. So far, the strike was peaceful. Men and women had been picketing at the entrances of the mill all morning. Not everyone had walked out, but we hoped there were enough people to make a difference. Word was coming in from across the region. Most of the Wheeling mills were closed, two were closed in New Kensington, and several Ohio mills were not operating. Unfortunately, many of the Pittsburgh plants remained open.

Sophie met me at the door with the girls and the neighbor widow. She bent down and kissed seven-year-old Mary on the head. "Now, you help take care of Elizabeth and be good for Mrs. Williams," she said.

"I will, Momma," Mary said.

"You two be careful," Mrs. Williams said.

"We will," Sophie said. "I'll be back by midnight."

It was no more than a twenty-minute walk down the hill to the mill. I was happy to see a large crowd of picketers along Moravia Street. When I came to America, I didn't expect to become rich, but I did hope to have a comfortable life. Struggling to feed and clothe my children was not what America promised, but it's what we got. I was determined that this strike would make a difference.

"There's Frank," Sophie said, pointing to a group of men and women along the entrance road. Deputies patrolled the gate beyond them.

We worked our way through the crowd. Frank had been there since 10 pm the night before and looked tired.

"It's a big turn out," I said.

"Four or five hundred," he said. "There was some name calling and rock throwing, but deputies are all over the place. We managed to convince some of last night's shift to join us. We'll see how many in the four-o-clock shift cross the picket."

"This is wonderful," Sophie said. "Is John still over at Hobart Street?"

"Yeah, with Dominic and Jim."

"Maybe I should go over there."

Men in overalls and short billed caps walked from the surrounding neighborhood toward the gate carrying lunch boxes. The strikers formed a line.

"We can use you here," Frank said.

A horn echoed across the valley, marking the shift change.

"Yeah," Sophie said. "Is there a barrel or something to stand on?"

Frank found a crate and positioned in the center of the driveway. He gave Sophie a hand up. She waved her arms at the approaching men.

"This is our time," Sophie yelled. "The people of the United States are watching us. It is on us to send a message to every worker across the country. We have voted for a gigantic protest. The leaders of this nation must understand who the steel fabricators of this country are."

A loaded streetcar approached from Moravia Street. The protesters tightened their ranks. A half-dozen deputies moved from the main gate with clubs drawn.

"Back away," a deputy yelled. "Let the workers pass."

Nineteen Nineteen 104

"If we are to have rightful pay and honorable working conditions, this fight must be won," Sophie continued. "We must stand against the oppressors, the capitalists, and the ruling classes."

The strikers stood firm.

We heard yelling in the distance. Men ran up Moravia Street.

"What's happening?" I asked.

"I don't know," Frank said.

Sophie continued with her speech.

John Simple was the first to reach us. "There's trouble at the other gate," he panted. "Someone took a Billy club and hit an officer over the head. Another officer was beaten. They're calling out the troops."

"Oh, my God," I said. "This is not what we wanted."

Like dry tinder lit by a match, the crowd erupted, throwing rocks and punches at anyone trying to enter. Sophie was knocked from her box. I struggled to reach her and helped her to her feet. Two innocent babes. It was all I could think. Sophie had children at home. She shouldn't be here. It should be me leading the way. I had less to lose.

"We have to get out of here," I said.

"No, Mary," she said. "We have to hold our ground."

Shots rang out from the guards at the mill.

Shots fired back from the strikers. Oh, no! Some of the men had guns.

I grasped Sophie's hand, but she tugged it away. "No violence!" she shouted. "We can do this peacefully."

Another volley from the guards shot into the crowd.

Sophie spun in place. Blood dripped from her neck. More blood bloomed across her skirt.

"No!" I caught her as she fell. No. No. No. This was not happening. She's a mother. Her children need her. My ears rang. My heart pounded.

Sophie sagged to the ground, eyes closed. More shots rang through the crowd. Men scattered.

"Frank!" I didn't see him anywhere. Had he been shot too? Was I going to be a widow? "Frank!"

"I'm here," he said.

"It's Sophie. She's been shot." I felt warm blood on my hands. "Why did this happen? It was supposed to be peaceful."

"She's going to be okay," Frank said. "We'll get her to the hospital."

A total of nine protesters were wounded that day: Sophia Johnson, John Simpel, Fred DiDano, James Kapsieles, Levi DePrano, Mrs. Mary Balzo, 7-year-old Virginia Conti, S. Esabella, and C. Galosz. Officers Fred Schuler and John Edwards sustained injuries, and a misfiring gun injured Deputy Chauncey Brown and Deputy D.R. Rolland at the courthouse. Approximately 100 protesters were arrested. Concealed weapons, including ice picks, clubs and guns were confiscated. Billiard halls were closed temporarily.

Sophie Johnson was pronounced dead from wounds to the neck and leg at 5:00 pm September 23, 1919. No procession was allowed at her funeral for fear that it would incite a riot by fellow strikers.

The 1919 strike lasted about six weeks and was considered a failure, but the struggle for social reform did not end. In 1922, at the prompting of President Warren G. Harding, U.S. Steel agreed to end 12-hour work shifts. Wages slowly increased. Steel Unions began to flourish in the 1930s.

Anthony Mangino

Lawrence County Courthouse

Martyred

By Betty Hoover DiRisio

Thomas J. Rocks (accompanying photo from his 1924 high school graduation photo) was born in New Castle to Hugh M. and Elizabeth Newman Rocks. The family lived on Wildwood Ave. "Tommy" attended St. Mary's School (1911-1920) and New Castle High School (1920-1924). He went to Holy Cross College (1925-1926) and entered the novitiate of the society of Jesus at Poughkeepsie, NY on August 14, 1926. Completing his novitiate in 1928, he took his classical studies there (1928-1930) and his philosophical courses at Woodstock College (1930-1933). For the next three years he taught at the San Jose Apostolic Seminary, the Ateneo de Manila and Sacred Heart Novitiate Manila, Philippine Islands returning to Woodstock in 1936 for his theological studies. With nearly fifteen years of preparatory education he was qualified to enter the priesthood. His ordination took place on June 21, 1939 at Woodstock, MD. Father Rocks said his first mass here at his hometown parish of St. Mary's on Sunday, June 25, 1939 with Father William F. Galvin and Father Leo S. Watterson, as decon and subdeacon.

After his ordination he returned to the Philippines and taught at the Ateneo de Cagayan, Cagayan, Oriental Misamis, Mindanao. Mindanao was one of the first islands in the Philippines to be attacked and invaded by the Japanese in December 1941. Local patriots, and American soldiers who refused to surrender formed a guerrilla organization that would later be referred to by General McArthur as the greatest resistance movement of the war. The Resistance fought on even after the surrender of Bataan knowing they could expect no immediate aid from the US Military. Father Rocks and fellow Jesuits became their spiritual fathers, adopting their cause and assisting in secreting the soldiers into the hills that the Jesuits had come to know so well.

While ministering to American soldiers in the jungles of Claveria, Father Rocks became ill with dysentery and was too weak to travel. A number of threatening men were seen approaching the soldiers' hut. The

Americans, having only one or two guns, decided to flee. But Fr. Rocks refused to join them, choosing to stay and guard their things. Rocks believed the attackers were Filipinos who would not harm a priest. He was dead wrong. The group of men were Magahats, pagans who lived in the mountains. Firing up through the bamboo floor of the hut, Rocks was killed instantly. The pagans then hacked up the priest's body, sacked the house and left. Father Rocks was killed on June 4, 1942. The returning American soldiers buried him in his vestments in the mountains. Father Rocks' parents had pre-deceased him, but he was survived by two brothers, Hugh of Waynesboro, and Edward J. of New Castle, and a sister, Ellen of Mercer, PA. (Account of his death found in "Guerrilla Padre In Mindanao" By Edward Haggerty, 1964)Betty Hoover DiRisio

Thomas J. Rocks
from 1924 high school yearbook

The Gauntlet

Jere Moon

I glance over my left shoulder, then quickly over my right. There they are. Lined up. Waiting. Taunting. My mouth feels drier than parchment. My heart quivers. So many. So many.

Decisions. Decisions. Which beverages do I choose at Beer4Less for my party tonight? I put two six-packs each of hard cider, light beer, and wine coolers into my buggy, and check out.

As I roll my cart across the parking lot, a man in crumpled clothing, who smells like wood smoke, tugs my arm. "Hey Lady..."

His hazel eyes behold a faraway look as he adjusts something on a string of leather around his neck. The breeze catches his flowing raven hair. "Can you spare a buck? I'm hungry." He holds out his palm.

"You're not hungry," I say. "You just want money to buy booze." I give him nothing, turn and push my buggy. I hate it when pan handlers lie.

Before I can reach my car, a stately eight-point whitetail emerges from the trees to grazes on the shrubs.

I stop my cart, reach into my purse for my phone, scroll to camera, and click. The perfect shot.

The buck drops.

"What?" I run to it and kneel.

An Indian brave dressed in buckskin leggings, moccasins, breechcloth, and a leather necklace of bear teeth, kneels beside me. He pulls the arrow out of the animal, wipes the point clean on the grass, and places the weapon into the leather quiver slung over his shoulder.

I strike the brave's muscular arm. "Why'd you do that? It's not hunting season."

THE GAUNTLET 114

He grabs me, and in a whirl, wraps hemp twine around my wrists, lifts the buck across his shoulders like a stuffed toy, and leads me away. Away. Toward the Shenango River.

I look back and see my phone drop to the pavement. There will be no calling 911.

The brave puts me inside a dugout canoe and places the deer on the floor of our vessel, gets in, and paddles across the river to the opposite bank.

Water droplets splash my face. *This is real.*

He beaches the canoe, gets out, and tugs me by the arm up the embankment. Drums pound. So does my heart.

Two boys dressed in deerskin, drag the buck from the canoe to their Matriarch who immediately starts skinning the animal.

I smell corncakes baking, sassafras roots boiling. I see long huts made of bark, cooking fires, and animal pelts stretched out to dry. Why haven't I ever noticed this village before? It's only a few hundred feet off West Washington Street.

Years ago, at a program at the Lawrence County Historical Society, I learned about an ancient Indian village located where New Castle is today. Wait until I tell the historians there that Kuskuski still exists!

The natives line up in two rows with a space between them. I know from reading Indian novels from the New Castle Library, that captives are forced to run the gauntlet to prove their worth. Will I be kept and adopted into their tribe, or painted black and burned at the stake?

Oh, how I long for one of those cold lite beers right now. I take a deep breath and center myself like I practice in yoga twice a week at Challenges.

The women each hold two clubs, the men only one. I know from taking thirty years of Aikido, at Demko Family Martial Arts located at Westgate Plaza, that women can be more ruthless than men. Men treat women like we are the weaker sex, but women look at other women like we are their competition. They want to take us out. This was going to be just as hard as running the 'gauntlet of belts' when I earned my black belt.

Someone lets out a war-whoop and shoves me into the swinging weapons. I deflect their attacks. I duck. I dodge. Their power goes by like the wind. My timing is impeccable. Sensei Demko would be proud. By the time I reach the end, I am so psyched, I feel like turning and running back through the gauntlet again.

But the brave who captured me from the parking lot at Beer4Less shoves me toward the chief.

I recognize the regal man—Chief Packanka. I met him once at a French and Indian war reenactment I attended at nearby Portersville Steam Show grounds. He nods with approval and gives a hand signal that resembled our OK sign.

Everyone, young and old, including me, starts belting out a song called, "*Where I Sit is Holy.*" I know the words well because, we sing it at the Spiritual Path Church of New Castle when we honor Native American beliefs.

By the last verse, everyone disappears, the way they do when our reverend says the final prayer—to celebrate the day--as the song goes.

I run to the dugout, get in, and paddle across the Shenango River, which I remember hearing at another lecture, is an Iroquoian word that means *beautiful one.*

When I reach the other side of the water, I get out, and run toward Beer4Less as fast as my feet will take me. Those exercise classes at the YMCA sure are paying off.

I find my cart right where I left it, my phone on the cement, still in camera mode. I click to gallery. The buck's still grazing peacefully, like nothing happened. Someone tugs my arm.

"Hey Lady..."

I turn and look into the hazel eyes of the man in the crumpled clothing. Is that a string of bear teeth around his neck? I quickly hand over a six pack of wine coolers that are still icy cold as when I bought them.

He lets out a war whoop and runs away toward the Shenango River.

All Clear

Kathy Hosler

Jagged bolts of lightning filled the sky as the railroad telegrapher tapped out the urgent warning....

"All Stop! Tracks ahead blocked," was the message Ernest Hosler sent to the B&O engineer who was racing along the rails in a steam engine pulling 18 cars.

A wicked summer storm had caused several huge trees to fall on the tracks south of New Castle and had brought all rail traffic into and out of the city to a standstill. No raw materials could get to the businesses. No finished products could leave.

The call for help went out, and men and boys came from the surrounding countryside to cut up and remove the offending trees. Men with crosscut saws and axes whittled away at the fallen monsters while boys cleared limbs and brush.

Once the tracks were again passable, word was sent to the UN Tower in West Pittsburg. Telegrapher Hosler relayed the *All Clear* message to the many waiting engineers from the B&O and the P&LE railroads. Wheels began turning, whistle blew, and the railroad was back in business.

In the early 1900's, there were very few cars or trucks. Almost everyone relied on horse and buggy for local transportation. The railroad was the main way of transporting goods and people throughout the country.

Years later, Ernest's son, Donald, joined him as a railroad employee. Don also became a telegraph operator. It was only natural as he had often accompanied his father to work and was 'fluent' in Morse code.

Don worked most of his career at the same UN train tower in West Pittsburg. Among his duties was keeping communications open with other towers along the tracks. He also delivered mail in a unique way.

Engineers have schedules to keep and there was no time to stop an entire train just to pick up a sack of mail. Instead, as the train barreled full throttle down the tracks, Don stood on the platform with a leather satchel crammed with mail. Using a long pole, he extended the satchel, and a crew member on the train snatched it as they passed by.

Trains carried more than mail, freight, and people. In the 1950's the circus came to town. Nearly the entire population of New Castle gathered along the tracks at the bottom of West Washington Street hill in the shadow of the huge Reddy Kilowatt sign. There they were spellbound as the heard the mighty lions roar and watched as elephants, camels, and other animals from the Ringling Bros. and Barnum & Bailey Circus unloaded from boxcars.

Continuing the family tradition, Don's son, Donald Jr. (Tiny) also went to work for the railroad. This was 1970. Gone were the smoke belching steam engines. Their replacements were sleek, powerful diesel locomotives that could pull more cars at higher speeds.

Commerce increasingly depended on the railroad as it crisscrossed the United States and beyond. Computers played a pivotal role in routing and operating the trains. Tiny worked in many areas and eventually became the Yard Master of New Castle and the surrounding area, not far from the UN tower where his father and grandfather worked.

Don't tell anyone, but it is rumored that on occasion some of the men would take two GP38's back-to-back to the Red Hot Restaurant in Ellwood City to get hot dogs. Back-to-back means that you hook two locomotives together, one facing each way. That way, one would pull them down to Ellwood City, and the other would bring them (and the hot dogs) back.

As fate would have it, Tiny's daughter, Gretchen, is also involved in the railroad industry. Gretchen is an engineer, but she doesn't operate trains. She's a mechanical engineer. Her specialty is to build and repair those impressive, high-tech engines.

One entire wall of her office is covered by a huge map of the world. On that map, there is a light denoting every engine in service, whether it is in New Castle, Pa.., Paris, France, or Tokyo, Japan. With the press of a button, Gretchen can see the exact location of each train, its destination, and whether there is trouble on the route.

Four generations (so far) of the Hosler family have helped keep the railroad operating in New Castle and beyond, first with a telegraph key and now a computer key. Their favorite message to send is still... *All Clear*!

The New Way

Stephen V. Ramey

Mary peered through binoculars from the roof of the Scottish Rite Cathedral. The city was in blackout, but lights from a single vehicle moved slowly down the hill at the south end of town.

"Motion on Sheep Hill," she said into her shoulder mic. "You hear anything?"

Paso's voice cut through a burst of static. "Could be Paul and Marenda. They've been having problems with their talkie batteries."

"Can't they just plug in? There should be a jack on the dashboard."

"Probably doesn't work anymore. That's the trouble with 25-year-old cars."

"I guess," Mary said. She raised the binoculars. The vehicle was a sedan. The headlights were too bright to see into the passenger compartment.

"Any ID?" Paso crackled.

"It's got to be them. They're on patrol. No way intruders make it through the barriers without us knowing."

"Unless they sneaked through on foot, overpowered our sentries, and stole their car."

Mary smiled. "Anyone ever tell you, you have a suspicious mind?"

"Guilty," Paso said. "Should I send up a drone?"

"No, give me another minute." It was easy to lose a drone at night and every asset was valuable.

"Well, check your ammo at least," Paso said.

Mary glanced at the gun rack where several AK-47s were housed. The weapons were kept oiled and ready, but she hadn't fired one in years. The community didn't waste bullets on target practice.

"We should manufacture our own batteries," Paso said. "Lordstown's QC has been pretty shoddy."

"That's advanced technology."

"Sure it is," Paso said. "Aren't we supposed to be aiming for self-sufficiency?"

"Yes, but—"

"No buts," Paso said. "It's the New Way."

Mary lowered the binoculars. She blinked. Staring into the light made her eyes sting. Paso was right, of course. You couldn't trust anyone but your own co-operative. Supply chains in the post-warming world were too damned fragile. Still, it seemed overwhelming at times. How were they ever going to be able to make *everything* they needed?

"We should exchange experts," Paso said. "You know, send a couple of our Ag gurus to them for a few months and bring in some folks who can show us how to refit one of the factories."

"Makes sense to me," Mary said. She yawned. Security was double duty. Everyone rotated through a few nights a month. In the morning she would be sorting produce from the East Side hydroponics gardens. It was remarkable what the ag-sci's had been able to grow. Pretty much anything they couldn't coax from the farmlands north of the city could be grown in these specialized greenhouses.

"Any luck?" Paso said.

Mary watched the car navigate a field of potholes on Jefferson Street. "They're nearing the Diamond now." She stretched her neck. "Did you know it used to be a priority to patch potholes?"

Paso laughed. "Sounds like someone's been talking to Aunt Barb."

"There's no avoiding it." Aunt Barb was always reminiscing. "I wish we could get her to be more forward-looking. She would fit into the community better."

"She *is* pretty old," Paso said. At 67, Aunt Barb was the oldest person in New Castle and the only one who could recall the cooperative's founding. Most elders worked as advisors. Aunt Barb knitted. It was a skill, Mary supposed, but not exactly one that made her irreplaceable.

"Should we alert Suze?" Paso said.

"We don't even know what's going on," Mary said.

"At the least they've violated protocol. Who's patrolling their section? Even if their two-way is malfing, there are others—"

"Just hold on for a few minutes," Mary said. "You know how Suze gets."

"Yeah, grumpy, but it doesn't last... usually." Paso sighed. "She's probably awake anyway. Those damn cats."

Mary chuckled. "They do catch mice."

"You ask me, they should go into the stewpot."

"Hey, hey, there's nothing wrong with a few pets. Caring for animals is a key trait of humanness. Don't forget you have a dog."

"Yeah," Paso said. "*A* dog. One. And he's an expert morel hunter, a net positive to the community. Cats, on the other hand..."

Mary went silent. Paso liked to argue. He'd advocate both sides of an issue if he had to. He'd never actually eat a cat. He was as vegan as the rest of them. Not that they had a ton of choice these days. The last deer the community had encountered was so emaciated by chronic wasting disease they'd had to burn it. While it had been predicted that the deer population in Western Pennsylvania would increase with climate change, scores of migrating flood and drought victims had pretty much devastated the herds within a few years.

"Progress?" Paso crackled.

Mary looked through the binoculars. For a second she didn't see the headlights, then they reappeared between trees lining Highland Avenue below the cathedral. She dialed the focus until Paul's profile came into sharp relief.

"It's them," she said. "Paul's driving, Marenda in the passenger seat." Mary squinted. "She's clutching a bundle to her chest. They both look a little… panicked, I guess."

"I'm pinging Suze."

Mary lowered the binoculars. "Yeah, maybe you should."

Suze was languishing in a strange dream. An Asian man dropped her off at a hotel that was infested with roaches and little mechanical dinosaurs.

"Suze?" Paso's voice sputtered over the speaker. "We need you at the cathedral." A red light blinked. "Suze," the speaker commanded.

"Yeah. Yeah." Suze threw back the comforter and grabbed the mic. "What now?"

"Sorry to wake you," Paso said. "We may have an incident."

"May? It damned well better be *do* have an incident if you're calling me at this hour." She took a flashlight from the stand and shone it on the clock across the room. *3:35.* Not as bad as it felt. She'd have to get up pretty soon anyway when the cats started their ruckus. She wasn't going to let Paso know that.

"I'm listening," she said.

Ten minutes later, Suze stood on the stone terrace of the sprawling Scottish Rite Cathedral. Several neighbors had already gathered near the sedan, and others were straggling in. It didn't take long for word to spread through the community even in the post-cellphone age.

An electric patrol car parked at the curb. The driver's door opened, and Eric stepped out. Suze nodded. He was a jovial, hard-working man, currently assigned to vehicle maintenance and night patrol.

"What happened?" he said. He slipped a handgun into the holster below his vest. "Paso wasn't real forthcoming."

"On my way to find out," Suze said. She flashed a grin. "Is Paso ever very forthcoming?"

Mike chuckled. "Enigmatic, I think he calls it."

As if on cue, Paso emerged from the lobby. His expression was less deadpan than usual, almost animated. A warbly wail sounded before the door closed.

Suze's pulse jumped. "Is that a... a *baby*?" There were no births scheduled for this quarter. Or next quarter for that matter. Crop yields were trending down. It was no time to bring on new mouths to feed.

Paso shrugged. "Marenda found it by the razor wire. Mother was dead."

Dread clenched Suze. "Did you call the reserve patrol?" They hadn't had problems with outsiders for a long while. Word was apparently out that the New Castle Cooperative defended its own, and the occasional herd of refugees just went around them to Canada. But that peace could end at any time.

"I called you" Paso said. "It's not an attack, just a mother and her kid trying to sneak in. Didn't quite make it."

"Christ," Suze muttered. "Of all the damned problems to throw at me now. Five days, Paso. Five more days and I rotate off the board."

"Could be worse," Paso said.

"How so?"

"You could've been the one to find the baby. Marenda's pretty shook up."

"Yeah... well..." Suze pulled open the heavy door and stepped into the lobby. Light threaded down from a line of solar-powered bulbs, illuminating a counter and snippets of dark red carpet. By day this was an imposing place, with twenty-foot-high ceilings and frescoed borders.

The baby continued to wail, the sound of its distress bouncing chaotically from surfaces unseen. Suze sighed.

The crying stopped. *Dead?* Suze thought before she could stop herself. She felt a burst of shame. There had been too much death in the past twenty years.

Marenda sat in a padded chair across the room. A sconce above her shone brightly, sucking down the solar batteries' precious charge. Paul stooped, bearded face pinched in concentration.

The stench of sour excrement wafted. It made Suze want to retch and laugh at the same time. How long had it been since she last experienced that smell? Too long. She remembered the trouble she had nursing her son. Even from this distance, she could see that Marenda was a natural mom by the way she held the infant. Too bad her husband had been jailed in the Poland, Ohio colony for trespassing.

"Paso tells me you found it inside the razor wire," Suze blurted. Paul and Marenda looked up together, Paul startled, Marenda calm.

The baby ramped up again. Marenda worked the tip of her finger into its mouth. Reluctantly, it started sucking. *It's so tiny*, Suze thought. It had to be a few months old but looked barely bigger than a newborn. How could something so small survive?

"You realize this is a problem," she said.

"We heard him crying," Marenda said. "I couldn't *not* investigate."

Of course, you could, Suze thought. *We've all done worse in our time.* She felt immediately guilty. She'd had her son before the quotas were enforced. Marenda would likely never get that chance. She wished Bret were here now instead of his assignment in the community's northernmost ag sector.

"What is this!" a brusque voice demanded. Suze turned to find Dennis charging toward them. He was a tiny man with weasel-like features and jutting chin, who had become an important figure in the community as a resource coordinator. Many looked to him for guidance.

"The situation is under control," Suze said.

"Is it?" Dennis glared at Paul. "Why is there a baby in our midst?" He pushed past Suze and leaned over Marenda. "Admitting an outsider without due process is an expulsitory offense." Marenda's eyes went wide. The baby rejected her finger and started crying again.

"It's just a baby," Paul said. He puffed out his full, bearish chest, forcing Dennis to take a step back.

Dennis threw his arms up. "Just a baby? *Just* a baby?" He slashed his hand downward. "What that *thing* is, is sixteen years of commitment. A consumer of resources we do not possess."

Paul grimaced. "You can't just leave a baby to die."

"Well, you damned well can't keep it here," Dennis shouted.

Suze's stomach clenched until she thought she might be sick. She had never been comfortable with confrontation. She glanced toward the door. A crowd had begun to condense around them, sleepy-eyed men and women in patched workpants. She relaxed a bit to see Mike among them. Sturdy, reliable Mike was a mechanical whiz and more than anyone's match. He would keep the tension between Dennis and Paul from erupting into violence.

Angela pressed through the crowd, looking composed and confident beneath a crown of curling blonde hair. One of a handful of people who did not have to rotate between assignments, Anglea had been their event coordinator for as long as anyone could remember.

"What's the problem?" she said in her deceptively sweet, innocent voice. She was neither sweet nor innocent, but one of the most well-versed people in group dynamics and management Suze had encountered.

"That," Dennis said, pointing. The baby blinked and yawned.

"I see," Angela said.

"It has to be disposed of. The sooner the better."

"And how to you propose we do that?" Suze said.

Dennis stroked his bald head. "Put it back. Let nature take its course."

"Now, Dennis," Angela said. "You can't mean that."

"You know the community statute as well as I do. Population has to balance production, or we all fail."

"I know what it says on paper," Angela said.

Suze looked up. This building must have been grand once. Now it reminded her of a gigantic skeleton, how they, the community, had taken up residence in the carcass of a glorious past. They were parasites, not builders. *It won't always be like this*, she thought. But it was difficult to feel that. She would certainly not live to see society's resurrection.

"Anyone who wants to throw this baby out will do it over my dead body," Paul said.

"That can be arranged." Dennis's face reddened. "Are you willing to give up your food shares for it? That'll be the day."

"I know a good way to make room for a baby," Paul growled. He started to draw his gun.

Mike glided forward and lightly grasped his shoulder. "I think we can agree to disagree here."

Paul grumbled, but withdrew his hand.

"Now, gentlemen," Angela said, "there's no need to do something drastic. We can discuss this issue like the adults we are."

"Some of us are adults," Dennis said. His glare shifted from Paul to Marenda. "And some of us are *emotional* thinkers."

Suze cringed. That echoed the shouts of her youth. *Socialist! Fascist! Emotional Thinker! Denier!* When all was said and done, those pegged deniers—which included her parents and most of their generation—had been executed or driven out of the cooperative. An image flashed of her father and mother embracing on their way to the firing squad. The experience had walled Suze off from her own emotions for decades.

"…how we survive!" Dennis yelled.

"What good is surviving," Suze said steadily, "if we become monsters in the process?" The words seemed to flow from a well deep inside her. "We've sacrificed so much. Must we also sacrifice our humanity?"

"Nothing is set in stone," Angela said. "This cooperative is run by and for the people. No matter what the charter says, it's always up for review."

"I move for a vote," Eric said.

"Seconded," another voice added.

"Absurd," Dennis said. "It's the middle of the night. There's no quorum."

"Then we'll start the vote," Suze said. "Do we have a recorder?"

A short woman stepped forward. "I can do it. I been sworn."

"Good" Angela said. "Aye to accept the child, nay to reject."

"I vote 'aye'" a shrill voice said. The crowd parted, allowing Mary's Aunt Barb through. A tattered knitting bag dangled from her left arm.

"You're crazy," Dennis said. "If we allow one exception, we'll allow a hundred. This community will never make it."

Aunt Barb smiled sweetly. "That's what they said when we formed the co-op. 'You won't make it through the first year,' they said. I still remember the mayor shouting from his pulpit." She nodded toward Dennis. "He fled to Florida after the riots. That was before it was wholly underwater, of course. You remind me of him a little."

"He was right," Dennis said.

"And yet, here we are." Aunt Barb crossed the room and sat primly in a chair next to Meranda. "We found a way."

"I vote 'aye'," Mike said.

"Aye!" Paul echoed.

"Nay!" Dennis shouted.

"Aye. Aye. Aye." A few Nays sprinkled in.

Aunt Barb retrieved knitting needles from her bag and settled back.

Dennis turned on her. "And, what, in God's name, do you think you're doing?"

"Booties," she said.

Al

Frank A. DeFelice

Where is Al?

This ubiquitous fellow can be found in all parts of New Castle. Whether one travels to the East Side, South Side, North Hill, West Side, Mahoningtown, or Downtown, Al can be seen in all sections of the city.

Who is Al?

When you know his last name, you'll recognize him.

It's Truism

Authors

Ann Abraham Antognoli was born and raised in New Castle, Pennsylvania. The sixth child of Lebanese immigrants, she learned to love storytelling as a child because her parents always told stories to teach life lessons. She earned a Bachelor of Science in English from Edinboro University of Pennsylvania and a Masters in English from Westminster College in New Wilmington, Pennsylvania. She taught high school English for over twenty-five years and lives with her husband David in New Castle, Pennsylvania. She and her husband are the parents of Jason, Erin, and son-in-law, Andy.

Kat Burg is best known as the former owner of the Burg Bar & Grill which she sold to retire. Now she enjoys life. She's presently writing a book, *Visits with Beverly and Others*. She is an active mother of two married daughters, Lisa and Amy. She is a certified teacher with a degree in K-12 and correctional education. Her degrees were earned from Geneva College and Slippery Rock University. She also taught at the Youth Development Center, Ellwood City School District, and retired from Neshannock School District as a learning support teacher after 22 total years of teaching.

Rowan Collins is a twelve-year-old student at Laurel Elementary School in New Castle, Pennsylvania. She enjoys reading, art, singing, and soccer. Rowan has been interested in photography for the past year. Her subjects range from local scenery to candid photos of her friends, pets, and siblings.

Frank A. DeFelice was born and raised in New Castle and graduated from New Castle High School. He attended Westminster College where he received a B.A. and then a Masters in Science and Education. He taught Spanish and World Cultures at Neshannock High School for more than 30 years.

Elizabeth Hoover DiRisio was born and raised in Lawrence County, Pennsylvania and graduated from Laurel High School. She attended

George Washington University in Washington, DC where she worked on mass tort (asbestos), toxic tort and tobacco litigation for the U.S. Department of the Navy and U.S. Department of Justice. She was also in charge of overseeing environmental compliance for the Navy's six industrial shipyards. Publications include *In Hot Pursuit-The Hidden History of the Underground Railroad in Lawrence County, Pennsylvania* (2016) and *Stage and Screen – The Historic Playhouses of New Castle, Pennsylvania Featuring a History of the Warner Brothers' First Theatre* (2016) "Betty" is currently retired and serves on the Boards of the Lawrence County Historical Society and the Historic Warner Film Center in New Castle while making her home in Fredericksburg, VA.

Kathy Hosler was born, raised, and still lives in the New Castle area. In 1971, she opened Kathy's Professional Pet Grooming which she operated for 46 years. At present she is a feature writer for two industry magazines, *Groomer To Groomer Magazine* and *Pet Boarding & Daycare Magazine*.

Dorothy Burchett Knight was born and raised in western Pennsylvania and is a senior citizen. She moved to New Castle from Knox in 2013 and quickly became adjusted to living here. She is married to Bob Burchett, and lives on Sunny Lane. She writes a weekly column for the *New Castle News* under that title. She has had several occupations through the years, from clerical, to restaurant work, to newspaper work and investigative work for a background investigation company. She taught religious education at St. Michael the Archangel Church in Emlenton. She previously wrote a column in the *Clarion News* in Clarion, PA, titled "On Huckleberry Ridge." Besides line dancing, her hobbies include dancing, reading, sewing and taking care of her two cats, Flopsie and Skittles. She loves to cook and have people over to share her creations. Dorothy has a daughter, a stepson and a stepdaughter. and six grandchildren. Her most recent collection is *Miles and Miracles* which documents a cross-country road trip she undertook at the ripe young age of 63.

Susan Linville received a PhD in biology from the University of Dayton and has lectured as adjunct faculty. As a freelance writer, she has published short fiction, newspaper and magazine articles, non-fiction books, and was a script writer for Indiana University's *A Moment of Science* Podcast Series. She has published three books on New Castle History including two volumes on historic homes (*Historic New Castle Neighborhoods, Vols. 1 and 2*) and a reference book on the Underground Railroad in Lawrence County (*In Hot Pursuit: The Hidden History of the Underground Railroad in Lawrence County, Pennsylvania,* with Elizabeth DiRisio). She owns the Pokeberry Exchange in downtown New Castle and manages Pokeberry Press, which helps people self-publish books.

Lavonne Lyles was born in New Castle and attended Shenango High School. She worked for Weinshanks Greenhouse and Reliable Luggage. Her interests include History, Gardening, and Poetry.

Anthony Mangino is a 35-year-old graduate of New Castle High School (class of 2002). He's been into photography now for several years, and has been the featured photographer in *The Watershed Journal* out of Brookville, Pa. He's also had photos selected to be the cover page for the *US Farm Report*'s Facebook page. He has a Facebook page for his photography (Introspective Images) and says, "I'm very grateful for the opportunity to contribute to a local publication that features local talent!"

Bev Martinko is a lifelong resident of Lawrence County and currently resides in Wilmington Township with her family. Her interests include spending time outdoors, photography, painting, reading, and a good Netflix binge.

Jere Moon is currently writing a historical romance set in pre-French and Indian war times about a French fur trader who falls in love with the woman he brings home to raise the son he kidnapped from its Native American mother.

Marcelle Neumann is a published author and freelance writer living in rural Northwest Pennsylvania. She is a member of the Society of Children's Book Writers and Illustrators, the St. David's Christian Writers' Association and Pennwriters Inc. She has won awards for her work. She fosters cats and has thirteen of her own. Mrs. Neumann spends her time writing, remodeling houses and, as a caregiver for her husband who is a disabled veteran.

Stephen V. Ramey lives in beautiful New Castle, Pennsylvania with his multi-talented wife, Susan Urbanek Linville, and a herd of semi-feral cats. His short fiction (literary, fantasy and SF mainly) has appeared in dozens of magazines and online venues. His first two collections of flash fiction, *Glass Animals* (Pure Slush, 2012) and *We Dissolve* (Pokeberry Press, 2019) are available at the Pokeberry Exchange and online via Amazon.

Randy Ryan is a former power lifter who holds three Pennsylvania state records and a world record in the bench press. He has a Master's in English from Youngstown State University and lives in new Castle with his two dogs, Lilly and Grizzwald. He has published children's (The Hunter series) and horror fiction (*Perspectives* and *Haunted Farms*) and is working on a new one (*Mediums*).

Debra R Sanchez has moved over thirty times and has lived in five states in two countries...so far. She and her husband have three adult children, five grandchildren, and a dog and a cat. She leads writing groups and workshops and hosts writing retreats. She is the author of several award-winning books in English and Spanish. Her writing has won awards in various genres, including children's stories, poetry, fantasy, fiction, and creative nonfiction. Several of her other plays and monologues have been produced and published. Other works have been published in literary magazines, newspapers, and anthologies. She is also a translator (English/Spanish) and language tutor/instructor for Spanish and ESL. Visit her webpage: www.DebraRSanchez.com

Colleen Seegers is a small-town Western Pennsylvania girl with a love for reading, who dabble in story telling and writing from a young age. She worked for most of her career as a registered nurse in California but has now returned home to stay. She has published a book of flash fiction pieces entitled, *Snippets*.

Robert Stull grew up in Mahoningtown and still lives in the same house he was raised in. He takes care of his mother, saying, "she took care of me when I was young so I will take care of her as she gets old." He is a working man and has been since he was around 12 years old. He likes to write when a thought comes to mind. He has many poems on different subjects.

Jim Villani of Youngstown, Ohio is the founder and publisher of Pig Iron Press, established in 1973. His pursuits include writing, poetry, teaching, lecturing and community organizing. He has taught at colleges and school districts and is certified language arts teacher by the Ohio Department of Education. He is Treasurer of the Green Party of Mahoning County, State Central Committee member of Green Party Ohio, member of the Academy of American Poets, Sierra Club, Friends of the Mahoning River and the Pig Iron Poets.

Richard Yates holds a master's degree in Elementary Education and a Bachelor of Science Degree in Psychology. As a Meteorological Observer in the U.S. Army, he learned to appreciate that change is inevitable in both the weather and the human condition. Still, he maintains an unwavering loyalty to the ideals of social justice and the potential for love to win us over. His books include: *A Love Book, Greg, Placemat Poems and Vignettes*, and *Mom*.

Other Books from Pokeberry Press

IN HOT PURSUIT
The Hidden History of the
Underground Railroad
in Lawrence County, Pennsylvania

SUSAN URBANEK LINVILLE
ELIZABETH HOOVER DIRISIO

HISTORIC NEW CASTLE NEIGHBORHOODS

North Jefferson & North Mercer Street Hill

Susan Urbanek Linville

HISTORIC NEW CASTLE NEIGHBORHOODS

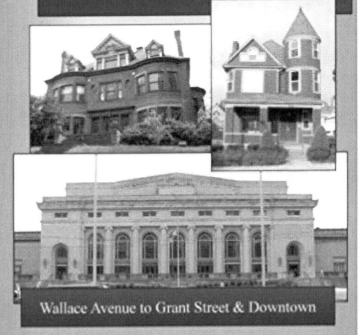

Wallace Avenue to Grant Street & Downtown

Susan Urbanek Linville

HAUNTED FARM

RANDY RYAN

Family, Farms & Battlefields:
The Nichols-Newlands and Gray-Heakins Families

What the Present Generation Owes the Past

John A. Nichols

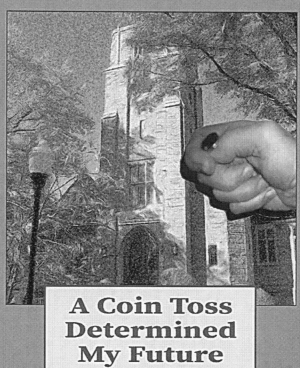

A Coin Toss Determined My Future
an autobiography

John A. Nichols

A Love Book

Richard G. Yates, Jr.

Snippets

Colleen Seegers

We Dissolve
Post-Progressive Fictions

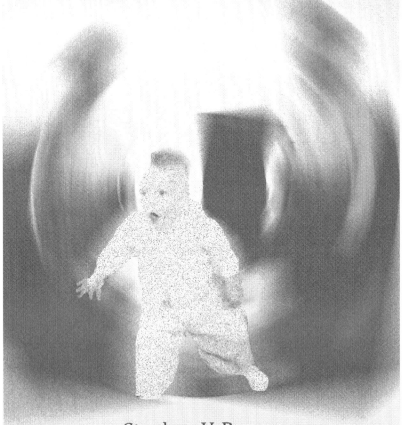

Stephen V. Ramey

Made in the USA
Lexington, KY
19 November 2019